The HOT Plan™

- Bolster Team Power
- Mobilize Responsibility
- Multiply Productivity
- Increase Engagement

By Harvey R. Dean, EdD

With C.L. King & Cody White

EDUCATION BLUEPRINT PUBLISHING

Education Blueprint Publishing
915 E Jefferson
Pittsburg, KS 66762
educationblueprintpublishing.com

Book Layout © 2014 BookDesignTemplates.com

The HOT Plan/Harvey R. Dean. – 1st ed., revision one
ISBN 978-0-9972302-5-3

This book is dedicated to all the teachers and leaders that have supported the cause of helping students and others engage and apply all of their learning domains: the mind (cognitive), the attitude (affective), and particularly the application/hands-on domain (psychomotor).

But perhaps most of all, I dedicate this book to my family members for loving me and tolerating my calling, my dreams, and sometimes my crazy ideas; and to the hundreds of Pitsco employees who own the HOT Plan, thereby ensuring learning for millions and millions of students each year.

"All things work together for good to those who love the Lord…"
Desire to do good with your blessings!

ENDORSEMENTS

ENDORSEMENTS

"As someone who has seen firsthand the dynamic and game-changing success of Pitsco, I see this book as one that pulls back the curtain and reveals the magic. That magic is simple but powerful. Derived from coaching a struggling high school track team, the HOT principles are relevant to building culture and vision for the smallest business to the largest global company. Whether for aspiring entrepreneurs or corporate leaders, The HOT Plan™ *gives essential lessons that will make a difference in the top line, bottom line, and long-term viability of any organization. The wisdom presented in Dr. Dean's book is pulled from the pages of his life's journey; it is a wisdom that can only be gained through a lifetime of trial and error. I think you'll agree with me ... his experiences and his insights are difference makers ready for the taking."*

— Steven A. Scott, President, Pittsburg State University

FROM THE AUTHOR

In many ways, this book provides a tour of my life.

The HOT Plan™ *is an organizational compendium of embedded keys and how-to elements. Because of a lifetime of experiences with HOT Plan ideas, I can say with confidence that the content and stories of* The HOT Plan *apply to* all *organizations. For example, when I first developed the HOT Plan, I moved the locus of responsibility to aspiring track athletes ... and they began to win, and win some more!*

When the HOT Plan was later applied in thousands of middle school education programs via our Synergistic System of teams, students became engaged and successful.

And when I utilized the HOT Plan within my business, the company was transformed into a highly engaged culture of dedicated and goal-focused employees, launching our business to continuing new heights!

If you are committed to the success of a business, an athletic team, or an organization, measurable success is within your grasp by applying the principles and processes provided in this book. Regardless of application, The HOT Plan *can revitalize and invigorate any organization.*

TABLE OF CONTENTS

Part I. HOT Beginnings

Chapters

1. Opportunity Knocks

2. Culture Happens

3. Ownership Matters

4. The HOT Plan

5. Success Shared

Chapter One

Opportunity Knocks

Weleetka High School never had a track team – in fact, the school never even had a track.

Weleetka sits in Okfuskee, at the time one of the poorest counties in the state of Oklahoma. Since many students in Weleetka had not traveled beyond the county line, offering a track team at the high school would not only give kids a new sports opportunity, it would also broaden their horizons by sending them out of the county to compete. I was a first-year teacher in Weleetka and my enthusiasm was unjaded. When asked if I would coach Weleetka's first boys' track team I didn't even have to think about my answer. My answer was simple and instant.

My answer was yes.

Tall boys, short boys, large boys, skinny boys – boys of different skin tones and various grade levels – pushed and crowded in line to sign up on the opening day of practice. In fact, nearly every boy in Weleetka High School came out for track that year, and eagerness was written on every face. Clearly, there was a wellspring of enthusiasm to be tapped in Weleetka. And, in the midst of the hopefuls, there were actually a few natural athletes.

Flush with vision and energy, I was as excited as the students. But how could we have guessed the struggles that lay ahead of us? Or that the idea that helped us overcome those struggles would guide my work for the rest of my life?

As a high school student, I loved running track. With fairly long legs, I ran the hurdles well enough to pull in a number of second-place medals. First place in hurdles usually went to our team also, thanks to a fellow runner who was also gifted in running hurdles. The competition between us could have been problematic, but the two of us managed to create a friendly rivalry that pushed us to excel. Our high school team enjoyed a camaraderie as we rode to and from the meets in the coach's car.

It seemed oddly too soon now for me to be the teacher and head coach of a fledgling high school track team in Weleetka. My ambition was for every student to taste the joy and success of the sport. I coached exactly as I had been coached. My first year's standard practice went something like this: First, the team jogged four laps around the football field. I ran them hard. Then, the group split – athletes could either work on individual events or wait for additional instruction from me. With 35 students on the team, it was nearly impossible to coach them individually, so – just like most coaches – I ended up focusing on the better athletes. Runners who weren't so talented got little guidance from me that first year.

> *Our shining opportunity for success turned to disappointment and frustration.*

Before long, it showed. Our shining opportunity for success turned into disappointment and frustration. Individual runners won a medal here and there, but not many, and the team did not gel. And as things turned out, I didn't just run the boys hard – I ran many of them off. Most of the boys who had signed up for the team dropped out before the season was over. Of the 35 kids that started, only eight or nine finished. We certainly did not win any track meets.

At the end of the first season, frankly, I knew I had failed. But why? How could these mistakes be fixed next year? I coached as I had been coached. This coaching method had worked for me as a student; why didn't it work for them? The joy and success in the sport that I had dreamed of giving my athletes didn't happen, and that stung. As the summer stretched out before me with the prospect of another painful track season awaiting us in the next school year, I needed some expert advice.

In those days the name on the lips of every aspiring young runner in the country was James Ronald (Jim) Ryun. He was a runner from Kansas – a regular kid who developed into a brilliant athlete. By age

17, Ryun ran a mile in less than four minutes, the first high school athlete to break the record. After high school, Ryun went on to Kansas State University and continued his training under the famous track coach Bob Timmons. If anyone could give expert advice on coaching runners to success, it would be Timmons. But would he talk to me – an unknown first-year coach teaching in one of the poorest counties of Oklahoma? I decided to reach out and mustered up the courage to give him a call. No answer. I left a message inviting him to call me back.

It seemed like an eternity, waiting and hoping for his return call. But one day, not really all that long after I left the message, my phone rang.

Bob Timmons – the coach of Jim Ryun, the first high school athlete to run a four-minute mile – took my call.

"Hello? May I speak with Harvey Dean?" a voice said. "This is Bob Timmons."

I stopped everything and stammered out my situation.

Timmons was a great mentor. He was willing, helpful, and eager to share with a beginner coach. He shared the title of a book with me that he claimed was the best resource for training runners. The nearest place the book could be purchased was at the Oklahoma State University bookstore in Stillwater, about 110 miles from Weleetka. It seemed like a long drive just to pick up a little book. But if this book held the key to my team's success, I was willing to make the drive. My heart raced when that small, spiral-bound book – the one that promised to hold the answers to my predicament – was safely in my hands.

The book described the Fartlek method of athletic training, which originated in Sweden in the 1930s. The system was fairly simple. In essence the Fartlek method – which means "speed play" in Swedish – is a training method that blends continuous training with interval training. Fartlek emphasizes catering workouts to each athlete's specific needs and event preferences. The approach was designed to be individualized and comfortable yet challenging. Reading through the little book from cover to cover, I was deeply impressed by the values the training method was built upon. The system empowered athletes to manage their own practice time and placed a great deal of control for the practice routine in the athlete's hands.

But what was the role of the coach? The Fartlek system improved athletic performance, but it didn't absolve me of the responsibility to coach. In fact, the Fartlek system seemed to require even more individualized attention than other methods. How was it possible to meet the demand?

Suddenly, I had an epiphany. At first the idea was small. But this small idea had the seed of a bigger idea buried in it, one that would incubate quietly for now and blossom much later in my career journey. My little idea was this: use 3" x 5" cards to give individualized training directions, with a separate card for each athlete. These cards, distributed daily, would have workout guidelines for each athlete's specific events. The cards provided individualized workout and training instructions for Monday, Tuesday, and Wednesday. Since each student could take charge of their own workout with the help of these cards, I was free to mingle, observe, and coach individuals on those days. On Thursday we switched to team practice, working on components such as hand-offs, starts, and various individual event tweaks. Friday was our day for group wind sprints, starts for runners, and light workouts for jumpers and throwers.

The new school year began, and having a new plan in place felt great. But convincing the boys to give the track team another try was my first hurdle and my first lesson in leadership humility. I had to face my mistakes and be up-front with the kids about them.

"Expect something altogether different next season," I said. "This year we are coming home with medals."

To my relief they extended their faith again and most of the boys in the high school came back out for track the second season.

I also made an additional deal with the students – a little act of faith on my part.

"If you work hard and follow the training instructions on the 3" x 5" card to the best of your ability," I announced, "I will enter you into several track meets – and you will medal this year. And if you don't medal at a meet, I will treat you to a milkshake for your effort." Weleetka was a poor community, and a free milkshake was a rare treat.

The deal seemed fair to the students. All the boys rejoined the team and got to work with their eye on earning a medal – or a milkshake.

In short order, the team had an amazing turnaround.

As the season unfolded, the boys made an amazing turnaround. Surprisingly, I bought very few milkshakes. The boys began to medal and eventually the Weleetka team began winning meets. Over the next three years, the Weleetka boys' track team won three conference meets and three regional meets and placed as runner-up for the Oklahoma State Championship in their division. In addition, one of our runners qualified for the USA Track & Field Junior Olympics and placed as one of the six fastest high school sprinters in the nation. Over the next three years, every athlete won at least one track medal during the season. Best of all, the students experienced pride and satisfaction in the sport, just as I had dreamed.

Even the sense of team unity grew under this training method. Being empowered within a structure of responsibility for their individual advancement somehow also fueled their sense of responsibility for the team, and the boys became each other's greatest source of support.

Those years as a young track coach taught me that trust, personal responsibility, and success walk hand in hand. Trusting the students to take charge of their own workouts with the aid of those 3" x 5" cards enabled them to trust me as their coach. Handing the athletes those cards moved the *locus of responsibility* – the power, instructions, and resources necessary to take charge of their own personal success – from me to them.

Taking the long view, the personalized training cards resonated with some deep truths I have since learned about human motivation. All organizations are collections of people dedicated to reaching a goal together. Therefore, all collective enterprises – from sports teams to schools to churches to corporations – can tap into these same basic human truths and multiply the productivity of their teams. *The system is the key.* And when a system for getting things done is aligned with basic human motivation, your organization will succeed.

Those years as a coach taught me that trust, personal responsibility, and success walk hand in hand.

Changing Education

A few years later, the need to create a culture of success again became obvious to me when I returned to Pittsburg State University in Kansas to pursue my master's degree in Education. In those days, many students were not motivated to learn in a classroom setting, and the educational system itself bore a good deal of responsibility for that. Students were regarded in a fundamentally wrong way – the same way I regarded my student athletes in that first year of coaching. As a beginning coach I was at the center of practices, telling everyone what to do. Similarly, traditional teachers were the center of the classroom, telling everyone what to learn, imparting knowledge primarily through lectures and assignments. This standardized, authority-centered method did not bring out the real potential of my athletes, and it didn't seem to bring out the real potential of students either.

> *Was there a better way for students to learn? The question wouldn't leave me.*

Was there a better way for students to learn? The question wouldn't leave me.

To find out, two fellow teachers and I began a business in Pittsburg to supply hands-on learning products for shop classes – the one curriculum area in schools that was dedicated to hands-on teaching methods. Our kits were popular, and we eventually graduated from the garage to an actual office and warehouse. Within a decade, Pitsco became a well-known provider of project-based educational products through catalog sales.

But there was still something bothering me about education; something deeper than products and projects.

I never stopped dreaming about how education might be different if only the system of delivering knowledge could be changed. What if students in the classroom could take charge of their learning with their teacher's guidance, like my athletes had taken charge of their practices with the guidance of their 3" x 5" workout cards? What if we moved the locus of responsibility for learning from the teacher to the students? What if students worked in teams, learning and applying what they had learned instead of taking notes on lectures and memorizing lists of facts for tests? What if content was project based, designed to come alive with real-world significance in the eyes of the students?

These questions and ideas burned in me until I left the classroom and devoted myself to finding the answers and creating alternative forms of learning through Pitsco. The more Pitsco provided kits and supplies for hands-on applied learning projects, the more I wondered if we could extend hands-on learning to core academic subjects as well.

In the 1970s and early '80s, the advent of affordable personal computers and video monitors finally provided a workable delivery system for technology-delivered modules of study. Once the Pitsco team could provide instructions and video demonstrations via teaching modules, teachers in these classrooms could shift to a new role. Freed from the demands of being the primary dispensers of information, they became the classroom experts, guiding student teams through the material. The results were exciting to both teachers and students.

Eventually, we extended this design to an entire curriculum and named it Synergistic Systems. Synergistic Systems curriculum moved the locus of responsibility from the teacher to the learner by combining content, technology, and projects. Technology provided the delivery system for information and gave students the tools necessary to take responsibility for their own learning.

Synergistic Systems was an instant success, and soon Pitsco Education was on its way to becoming a science, technology, engineering, and math (STEM) education leader. Today, Pitsco is the leading STEM curriculum provider in the United States and in 53 countries around the world.

We moved the locus of responsibility from the teacher to the learner.

Changing Business

Synergistic Systems took off quickly, and the Pitsco staff hit a dead run to catch up with the demand. Employee numbers shot up quickly to more than 100 people for the first time, and with a lack of warehouse space, we soon found ourselves in the middle of a mess. We needed to increase our efficiency. I hired an expert to come in and create greater efficiency in our company, but his leadership style turned out to be a bad fit for Pitsco's creative, entrepreneurial culture. The expert thought a top-down hierarchy was the answer. As he implemented a strictly top-down management style, the collaborative idea-sharing culture of Pitsco took a nosedive. My smart and creative employees felt their ideas were no longer welcome, and many said they felt helpless as they watched the company they loved slowly drift away from them. Once vibrant with friendship, creativity, and camaraderie, the Pitsco culture fractured, and mistrust multiplied. Motivation waned and productivity stalled. Top members of the leadership team and key employees began talking about leaving. My company, poised at the very edge of success, was poised at the edge of failure at the same time. We were in a full-blown crisis.

Looking back, it was really when things started going wrong that I began to see how they might go right. I thought back to the lessons learned from that first coaching experience and from the development and success of Synergistic Systems.

Very late one night while I was sketching solutions to my dilemma at the kitchen table, a plan suddenly fell onto the paper. The essence was simple: just as I had done with the track boys years ago and the kids in the classrooms, I needed to move the locus of responsibility for success. Instead of being in the hands of the managers and supervisors, the locus of responsibility belonged to the employees. Executive leadership would still clarify long-term vision and lay out the company's Must Win Challenges (MWCs), but employees themselves would be teamed up and asked to create targeted goals to meet those challenges. We would also reward employees for hitting their targets. I dubbed the plan scribbled on paper that night the HOT Plan. The HOT Plan was the beginning of the transformation of our company culture, our growth, and the secret of our continued success today. I let the efficiency expert go and immediately began to implement the first phases of the HOT Plan. As with my track team decades before, the turnaround began at once. Pitsco began to overcome the challenges that had threatened to undo the company.

The essence was simple: move the locus of responsibility from management to employee teams.

The success of the HOT Plan helped me recognize that the way many businesses think of their employees is just as flawed as the way traditional education thought of students. In the world of business, employees often are viewed as people who must be told what to do – not as intelligent, talented human beings with leadership potential. This viewpoint is unfortunate. Leadership potential exists inside every employee. What if every organization tapped into the full leadership potential of every employee and put it to work for their company?

The plan that fell onto paper at my kitchen table that night began my journey toward leading our employees toward their own leadership potential. Today, one of our company goals for all of our employees is to help them find their place of leadership at Pitsco and accept the locus of responsibility for their work. When the locus of responsibility is granted and accepted across an entire organization, productivity multiplies and engagement increases.

The HOT Plan has fueled our company's growth, excitement, and success for nearly 20 years now. The method has become the means by which we share responsibility for the vision but has also provided a structure through which we care for one another and reach out to our community. The HOT Plan has helped us build a great culture and carried us together toward the accomplishment of Pitsco's vision: *leading education that positively affects learners.*

Because the HOT Plan taps into the reservoir of natural human motivation, its potential and power extend far beyond our company boundaries. In fact, I would go so far as to say that everywhere a worthy vision exists, the HOT Plan can and will empower employees or team members to take ownership of that vision and bring it to pass.

Put simply, *The HOT Plan*™ can work for you.

This book is a practical, step-by-step guide to moving the locus of responsibility of organizational success from the hands of the management to the hands of teams and team members. The HOT Plan is not an untested theory. The program is backed by nearly 20 years of experience at Pitsco, Inc. and a growing body of research. Shifting your leadership structure from a top-down hierarchy to an agile and adaptive HOT Team system is a game changer.

The culture at Pitsco today is happy, engaged, and productive. One of my favorite activities these days is to walk around the campus, stop in various buildings, and visit with our staff. Whether I am in the Call Center, Shipping and Receiving, or Research and Development, the culture is consistent. We laugh a lot, share ideas, and genuinely enjoy each other. The HOT Plan has shaped Pitsco into a great place to work.

Put simply, The HOT Plan™ *can work for you.*

According to Liz Brashears, director of human capital consulting at TriNet Inc., "Culture is a business issue that has significant impact on a venture's ability to generate a return on investment and should be prioritized and measured just like other business objectives such as financial growth, product development, sales, marketing and the like." [1]

The HOT Plan is a powerful way to make sure your culture and your business are maximized for impact. Implement the HOT Plan, and your culture will shift from being a "business issue" to a business asset.

Chapter Two

Culture Happens

No matter how successful your company or organization is, if it lacks a healthy culture, it is not reaching its full potential.

Without that healthy yet intangible mix of trust, motivation, and shared responsibility among your members, justice will not be done to your organization's mission, whether the organization is for-profit, not-for-profit, religious, educational, athletic, or any other group of people bound together by a common goal or purpose.

Culture isn't easy to define. It is easy to talk about it in general terms – about the importance of creating a great company culture – but what is that, exactly? And how is it achieved? Is business culture quantifiable?

The clearly quantifiable aspects of business – the numbers on profitability, productivity, or employee retention rates – are fairly straightforward. The numbers tell the story. Culture, on the other hand, is more elusive. Clearly it exists, but it is often more sensed than quantified. How do we measure something we can't quite define? How do we address something we can't quite measure? The predicament is real.

In spite of growing numbers of studies that give evidence that a highly engaged company culture is the key to sustaining profitability, culture in many businesses is often expected to grow with little nurture or intention. Nothing could be more shortsighted in today's increasingly competitive marketplace than ignoring your culture.

Culture and effectiveness are inextricably linked.

Companies around the world are finding that to survive in today's competitive marketplace, they must invest in their culture and the branding of their company, not just in their products. Richard Mosley, a pioneering voice in the field of employer branding, says that leading companies not only "strive to deliver uniquely valuable products and services, they also seek to shape a distinctive organizational culture and brand identity."

"The shared behaviours and beliefs that define [business] culture can deliver significant competitive advantages," Mosley continues. "A strongly shared sense of culture and purpose can drive extraordinary levels of motivation, loyalty and performance."[2]

In the *New York Times* best-selling book *Change the Culture, Change the Game,* authors Roger Connors and Tom Smith agree that "Optimizing the culture should command your attention every bit as much as your effort to achieve performance improvements in manufacturing, R&D, sales, and every other organizational discipline."[3]

A lifetime of experience working in organizations and businesses has confirmed to me that culture and success are inextricably linked. Core HOT Plan values are based on the idea that a culture that fosters success will grant employees the locus of responsibility necessary to do their jobs well. But before we go any further, let's consider the culture in your business or organization.

Beyond the paycheck, what motivates your people to stay?

When you imagine an ideal culture for your workplace, what comes to mind? To visualize the optimum culture for your business, clear your mind of any immediate day-to-day concerns. Focus instead on the long view of your business – its structures, processes for getting work done, and the flow of communication. Think about how employees relate to the business and how they get work done. How do they relate to each other? Beyond the paycheck, what motivates people to be loyal to your company or organization?

There are three dominant cultures in the marketplace, with a fourth culture – a game changer – on the horizon. Which one best describes what you see in your mind's eye when you consider these questions?

The first three business cultures are likely to sound familiar. For the sake of discussion, let's call the first (and most familiar) business culture "top down," the second "decentralized," and the third "empowered." Bear in mind, however, that the fourth workplace culture, the "millennial" culture, is reshaping all three of the others. The millennial influence reflects a global shift in the workplace that some researchers are calling seismic. This shift is occurring as millennial-generation employees – those born after 1980 – become the majority of workers in the workforce. In the US, 63 percent of the workforce will be millennial by 2020, according to the US Bureau of Labor Statistics.[4] For companies that employ international workforces, the numbers are even higher. For example, the global financial services company PricewaterhouseCoopers (PwC) reports that 80 percent of its worldwide workforce will be made up of millennials by 2016.[5]

Millennial culture is reshaping the way we conduct business.

What does this mean for workplace culture? Millennials are more technologically savvy and generally better educated than earlier generations, according to the US Chamber of Commerce study *The Millennial Generation Research Review*.[6] The review reports that the millennial cohort – which it estimates at 80 million people in the US in 2012 – is the first generation to grow up digitally fluent on the Internet, in both their professional and social life. Millennials bring more of a cultural shift to the workplace than digital fluency. Because of their lifetime of experience with online global connections, their perspective is influenced by international friendships, digital access to information, and creative team-based collaborations on the web. It is impossible to overestimate the influence of this cultural shift on the workplace of the future.

Top-Down Culture

Returning to premillennial workplace traditions, a top-down hierarchy is unquestionably the primary workplace culture that emerged from the industrial age. Top-down business culture provides strong direction from the top, or executive, level and provides very little autonomy for employees. In this type of management approach, the flow of communication is primarily vertical.

Top-down culture sends the message, "Stay in line."

In a top-down culture, the executive leadership of the organization owns all the decisions, and communication and power flow from the top with little opportunity for communication to flow up from the bottom. The business is organized into a hierarchy; work goals and direction are generated by C-executives (CEO, CFO, COO, etc.). Changes in policy are handed down as directives, often with little explanation. Most employees have no idea who decided to change things or why.

A top-down culture does not expect or empower its workforce to provide input that would affect the organization itself. The unstated message of a top-down culture seems to be "Stay in line." This is easily seen in the communication flow of the organization. Since communication flows from the top down, there are few established lines of communication for employee input. In some top-down organizations, suggestion boxes are made available, but these suggestion boxes are often regarded with a sort of wry skepticism.

Although supervisors are better positioned to have influence in the hierarchy, they often hesitate to bring up new ideas as well. If suggestions are innovative, unusual, or tamper with how things are done, the supervisors are especially hesitant. The idea of implementing any sort of change without express permission is unfathomable to mid-level managers and supervisors in top-down companies.

When faced with a problem to solve at work, employees of top-down organizations look to someone else to solve the problem instead of taking care of it themselves. Who wants the responsibility – or the blame – if things go wrong? This becomes a problem when small glitches in the work process that could be nipped in the bud continue instead until they reach the proportion of a management-level crisis.

> *It is not surprising that employees often express feeling stifled in top-down organizations.*

It is not surprising that employees often express feeling stifled in top-down organizations. But how employees feel was not an issue to be considered when this hierarchal form of business culture was developed. Hierarchal culture was birthed in the age of the factory, at the dawn of the industrial revolution. Although many today argue that the age of the factory is dead, the hierarchal top-down culture lives on. In fact, it is still, unfortunately, very common.

Decentralized (flat) Culture

The second type of business culture is designed to move away from the factory-based top-down model and into the 21st-century workplace.

Decentralized, or flat, culture advocates that top-down leadership must surrender to an open give and take between C-staff, supervisors, management, and employees. In flat culture, leaders embrace an inclusive style of leadership that shares responsibility between the management and the employees.

Flat culture advocates inclusive leadership that shares responsibility.

Decentralized culture is much touted these days. In an ideal flat culture, employees and supervisors operate with "an unobstructed flow of corporate commonality," according to former teacher and globally recognized leadership expert Dan Pontefract in his book, *Flat Army: Creating a Connected and Engaged Organization.*[7] Pontefract advocates for a "culture of borderless collegiality." It is a workplace culture built on a high level of trust between employees and management. Communication flows easily between workers and management by design; problems are expected to be solved collaboratively.

But an unintended result in some flat organizations is a lack of visionary leadership and unified direction. How much direction can the C-staff give? If employees have autonomy, who sets the direction of the company? How are key initiatives and goals decided? Human nature looks to leadership for vision and direction to give parameters for the enterprise. If leadership is not confident and clear about what needs to be accomplished and vision is not spelled out, employees begin to suspect that perhaps there is no vision at all.

Without a clear and compelling "why" to the work and an all-encompassing, ennobling vision, subtle chaos can spread throughout the limbs of the organization. Work efforts in various departments might fail to sync or may even contradict each other. Without a big picture painted by company leadership, individual departments cannot visualize their relationship to the whole. Unless company vision and strategic initiatives are clearly stated, employees do not know how to target their work. In the end, some employees in flat organizations have told me that though they prefer flat culture to a hierarchy, freedom without direction is, in its own way, also stifling.

> *Autonomy without direction, however, produces a subtle chaos.*

In its most extreme case, flat culture can lead to a growing sense of purposelessness. Unless a decentralized culture is guided by targeted goals and a unified vision, employees might gain autonomy but do not yet have the locus of responsibility needed to reach their full potential along with their newfound freedom.

Empowered Culture

A third type of organizational culture is empowered culture, a culture in which members at all levels experience clarity of vision, autonomy, and responsibility. In an empowered culture there is strong leadership at the top, but the structure is flexible, team based, and targeted for results. Vision, along with essential company challenges and key initiatives, is clearly communicated. Communication is the oxygen of such a structure; it flows in and out of all levels like breathing.

Company direction comes from the top but is developed by an active leadership team that represents every segment of the company. Input from employees is a valuable resource. Once the executive leadership team identifies the annual goals and strategic initiatives, the department supervisors and interdepartmental team leaders become primary communicators and coaches to their own departments and teams. They coach their teams to identify goals that fit into the larger plan. Because employees are involved in targeting and planning their work, they take ownership in it and become invested in the success of the company. Most employees in empowered systems are rewarded with some type of bonus that enables them to share in the company's success.

> *Empowered culture has strong direction, flexible structure, and team-based accomplishments.*

Employee input is vital in an empowered culture; everyone has skin in the game. The success of the employees at their individual tasks and the success of the company are directly linked. Innovation is encouraged. Ideas, even radical ones, are welcomed. People not only feel empowered to solve their own problems, they are expected to do so.

Motivation in an empowered culture flows naturally from shared interest. Employees empowered to target their own outcomes based on the company's strategic initiatives become partners in carrying the burdens and celebrating the successes of the company.

There is a key to creating a successful empowered culture; without it, the empowered culture will not function. An empowered culture requires an intentional, workable system that provides accountability and coordinates all of the moving parts. At Pitsco, the HOT Plan provides that system and has sustained our empowered culture for nearly 20 years.

Millennial Culture

What impact is the millennial generation expected to have on the business cultures that exist in the marketplace today?

Something akin to the seismic shift of an earthquake, says PwC. When the millennial generation entered the global workforce in the early 2000s, they quickly demonstrated that they had different expectations and motivations than previous workers.

Millennials are bringing a seismic cultural shift to the business world.

PwC reports that within 10 years after their company hired its first millennial-generation workers, the millennials were leaving the company in alarming numbers. When PwC tried to entice them to stay with traditional benefits and long-term incentives, millennials were uninterested. What was going wrong?

The leadership of PwC attributed this tidal wave of resignations to a cultural shift. With an expectation that 80 percent of its worldwide workforce would be millennial workers by 2016, PwC commissioned a qualitative and quantitative research study. The study, conducted in 2011 by the University of Southern California and the London School of Business, examined millennial workplace motivations, values, and expectations. The study drew from the PwC worldwide employee base, and 18 global territories participated with 44,000 web-based surveys providing the foundation of data. Additional face-to-face research was drawn from direct interviews, focus groups, and online "jam sessions" between employees and PwC leadership. Released in 2013, the report, *NextGen: A Global Generational Study*, claims to be the "most comprehensive global generational study" to date.[8]

The conclusions drawn by PwC analysts supported the idea that the hierarchal systems of the industrial age and their derivatives are no longer functional in today's world. If companies hope to compete for the best talent of the future, they must change.

The HOT Plan helps traditional businesses assimilate millennials.

The PwC study uncovered a paradigm shift in millennials regarding where and how to make a living. In the millennial paradigm, work can be done from anywhere, and long-term loyalty to one company is unnecessary. The study says millennials are looking for:

- "Work that is interesting and meaningful."
- Opportunities to work internationally.
- Flexibility at work that matches life changes.
- Team-based work environments.
- "Transparency … as it relates to … careers, compensation and rewards."
- "Input on their work assignments."
- Frequent recognition for their accomplishments.[9]

Although the HOT Plan was developed before the millennials entered the workforce, it is interesting to us that the HOT Plan meets all of these millennial expectations. Perhaps this is because the program was designed for a creative and entrepreneurial workforce from the start. Or perhaps because the system breathes with communication from all directions, we have been subtly adapting our company to millennials without realizing it. Regardless of the reason, of this we are confident: the HOT Plan is working well in our traditional business, and it will work in yours. The program provides a proven and affordable path for traditional business to adapt to the millennials.

A Different Culture

To give a sense of perspective, it is important to share that although the culture at Pitsco today is positive and empowering, it wasn't always this way. Prior to 1997, Pitsco had what you might call a "single-source answering protocol."

OK, I admit it. This is just a technical way of saying that I was in the middle of everything and all project decisions came through me.

This protocol was not really planned in a formal way. In fact, we hardly had a formal structure at all in those days. It was simply that as the owner with a strong vision and all the company debt, I needed to be in charge.

Of course, Pitsco was smaller then, and it was still possible for me to know everyone and get their input about the company's operations. There was a lot of collaboration, even if I was the final decision maker. We didn't exactly fit the top-down model, because I welcomed creativity. If someone had an idea, they came directly to me and we hashed it out. But I was the one to say yea or nay. We called it our "spiderweb structure," and I was at the center of that web. It was a lighthearted description, but as our operating structure, it was pretty accurate. My passion for *leading education that positively affects learners* radiated from the center of the web, and everyone seemed to share that same passion. I fueled the passion for employees, for teachers, and for students.

When our flagship curriculum product, Synergistic Systems, was developed, I saw its larger potential and made the decision for the company to produce and promote it. This decision wasn't based on cost or a marketing analysis study or potential sale numbers. It was a purely idealistic decision that thankfully proved to be pragmatically sound. I knew it was the right thing to do for education, so I gave the go-ahead and we launched it. The costs, growth, and alterations of the products skyrocketed, but the catalog sales of our curriculum and other products grew as well, and those profits supported the investment needed to continue developing Synergistic Systems. Synergistic sales took off and remained our lead product for many years, proving the decision was a sound one. A lot of my decisions were like this – based more on gut instincts than on statistics and numbers. Although not every decision worked out, the overall model of "Harvey Dean, Decider-in-Chief" worked. At least for a while.

As I mentioned in Chapter 1, we grew to about 100 employees and our way of doing things began to fall apart. To be quite honest, I didn't want to give up my spot in the center of the web of activity. I loved the role of being in the middle of it all and being Chief Decider. But the vision was now too big for one person to carry. If the company was to grow, the structure had to change.

At first, I didn't quite know how to make that change and gave away too much leadership too quickly. The new leadership I brought in changed the structure too drastically.

Under the new leadership style, valued people in the company began to express a growing distress.

> *We needed to build a culture of empowerment, ownership, and accountability.*

Once I thought about it, I quickly realized that instead of more top-down leadership, we needed the opposite. What we needed was a system and structure that would move the locus of responsibility for Pitsco's success out of my hands and into the hands of everyone in the organization. We had to create a program that would build the culture of empowerment, ownership, and accountability necessary for our organization to flourish. On top of that, there was no time to reinvent the wheel – the system had to work within our more or less standard company structure of departmental divisions that already existed.

The solution to our dilemma, which we came to call the HOT Plan, has been continually refined for nearly 20 years now. In addition to helping us reach our company goals, the HOT Plan transformed our company's culture.

A Culture of Purpose

One of the secrets of the HOT Plan's success in building a great company culture is communication that helps employees connect their individual work to the result – the full impact of your product or service and the world it serves.

> *Millennials point to supporting a cause as a deciding factor when choosing where to work.*

For some companies and organizations, their product or service makes a significant social impact. For others, a portion of company profits is openly dedicated to supporting a social cause. Employees can observe that as profitability increases, company contributions also increase, and their loyalty to both the cause and the company grows. In fact, many are motivated to work harder on behalf of the company so that more is contributed. Supporting a cause is so important to millennials that it is named as a deciding factor by them when faced with choosing between employers.[10]

There are many ways to involve your business in a larger purpose, but however you accomplish this, make sure your employees have a chance to see your company's good works in action.

One summer morning we did this in a unique way at Pitsco. We sent more than 50 Pitsco employees off at the crack of dawn on a road trip to an event where they could see their work put to the test. Would the products they had designed, manufactured, and shipped stand up under pressure? They were about to find out.

Chapter Three

Ownership Matters

I n the wee hours of the morning just before sunrise, a sizable group of Pitsco Education employees – nearly 50 of them – gathered in a darkened Pitsco parking lot to board a chartered bus and head for St. Louis, Missouri.

The journey to St. Louis was a paid day off for the employees, sponsored by Pitsco so they could attend the *FIRST*® Championship, a robotics competition sponsored by the *For Inspiration and Recognition of Science and Technology* foundation (*FIRST*) of Manchester, New Hampshire. *FIRST*, a 501(c)(3) not-for-profit public charity, "designs accessible, innovative programs that motivate young people to pursue education and career opportunities in science, technology, engineering, and math."[11]

We want employees to have a firm sense of the power and purpose of their work.

St. Louis is a long road trip from Pitsco. It is about a five-hour journey and the breadth of an entire state from Pitsco's home campus in Pittsburg, Kansas. But this road trip was truly free for the employees; there was no trip expense to those attending and no obligation to work on Pitsco's behalf at the competition. There was one reason Pitsco sponsored the journey and one reason alone: to provide an opportunity for employees to witness firsthand the results of their work. Students from all over the world were gathering in St. Louis to compete in robotics, and Pitsco TETRIX® robotics was one of the systems chosen for the competition. In fact, it was the design platform of choice among young robotics engineers at the high school level, along with robotics products from LEGO® Education, a long-standing robotics partner with Pitsco.

The atmosphere of the competition pulsed with the high-voltage energy of bright young minds at work. At robotics competitions, students launch their mechanized creations to face off with other robots, all vying for the title of best in completing a specified task. The original design-and-build aspect of the competitions provides an unbeatable educational opportunity for students. As a reward for the students' effort, *FIRST* always provides first-class entertainment for the awards celebration.

That spring was no exception. *FIRST* had brought in a well-known hip-hop band, the Black Eyed Peas, featuring the American rap artist will.i.am for the celebration. This group was such a strong draw that their presence guaranteed the *FIRST* competition its own hour-long special on prime-time network television. The robotics awards ceremony filled the Edward Jones Dome at America's Center in St. Louis with blaring music and the voices of thousands of cheering students and their sponsors.

Emotional connection to work determines one's personal investment in it.

But what mattered most to Pitsco employees was not the high-energy excitement. It was, instead, the quieter moments – the moments when students were knitting their brows as they knelt over their robot troubleshooting last-minute problems or when students from different nationalities met and communed over their shared fascination with engineering and technology. It was the moments when middle school kids mastered seemingly impossible skills and grew in self-confidence before our eyes. These were the quiet and small miracles of discovery that undergirded the event, and it was important that we, as a group, witnessed them together. As Pitsco employees, we all played a part in setting the stage for these miracles of learning. In many cases, it was Pitsco products that made all of those quietly profound moments possible.

When the bus finally rolled back into our parking lot in Kansas late that night, 50 sleepy employees drove home changed by what they had experienced. They had looked into the eyes of the students, the people to whom we are most accountable, and glimpsed what was at stake when our products are put to use. Our employees came face to face with the purpose and power of their work.

Ownership Requires Purpose

The experience of purpose is foundational to being human, as real as the desire to feel love.

Some shrug at such pronouncements, but we have all heard the personal stories of those who claim that discovering a solid sense of purpose changed their lives. Often they proclaim, "I didn't realize what I had been missing!"

Organizations too are changed by gaining a solid sense of purpose. It is purpose that feeds the faith and passion of people in any organization. Owning that purpose forges a deeper connection between your team and your vision.

In his book *Drive: The Surprising Truth About What Motivates Us*, Daniel Pink collects half a century's worth of behavioral research showing that across all age groups and cultures, the creative and emotional connection workers feel with their work determines the depth of their investment.[12]

People generally want to know their work connects them to something larger than themselves. This is as true in a for-profit company as it is in a charity organization. There are at least two important ways this comes into play in the workplace. The first is motivation – the desire employees feel to fulfill the company's vision if they are proud of what they do. The second is self-esteem – the sense of value which comes from seeing that one's personal contribution to the company matters.

Purpose is the cornerstone of your company culture. Incentive programs, soft-skills training, and team-building exercises are good tools, useful for building a positive culture in your business, but they are just that – tools. Purpose is more than a tool; it is the clay from which your business culture is molded.

> *Purpose feeds the faith and passion of your people.*

As an education company, we have a leg up on pursuing a purpose that employees find easy to love. Since almost everyone loves to help kids, the nobility of our purpose isn't a hard sell. But perhaps your company's purpose is not quite so easy to love. Even if it is not flashy, the products or services your company provides make a difference in the world they serve. Showing your employees what that difference is and helping them understand your company's mission and vision will help your employees believe in your company.

The simple fact is that most people take greater ownership of their work when they can embrace its purpose. This is especially true for millennials, who want to feel connected to and invested in work that has a greater impact on the world. When employees embrace the purpose of the company they work for, their work has the potential to transform from adequate to inspired.

Ownership and Belonging

A second connection to ownership among your employees grows out of the basic human desire to belong to a group.

Humans are social creatures. Most people want to be individuals, yes, but individuals within a community. Belonging to a community is of such great importance that once people join a group, most become willing to sacrifice personal time and energy for the success of that group. Your company as a whole, if well managed and dedicated to a noble purpose, can benefit from this inherent tendency.

People want to be individuals, yes, but individuals within a community.

A sense of belonging happens best for most people in the smaller groups within your company, such as individual departments or cross-disciplinary teams. The need to foster that sense of belonging is one of the reasons that the HOT Plan is a team-based plan.

The HOT Plan is designed to turn all eyes toward shared goals that we identify as HOT Targets (HOTs). The plan is intentionally crafted to build community. Although it is true that a team-based plan is more efficient than an individualistic approach in a number of ways, efficiency is not the main reason we based the HOT Plan in teams.

Harnessing the energy and desire of employees to belong to a group does not take away from their individuality. If teams are properly chosen and led, individuality remains intact because each member is chosen to be on the team *because* of his or her individual skills, style, and/or perspective. When employees know that their personal competencies are the reason they are chosen for the team, it strengthens their sense of individuality.

By design, the HOT Plan builds community.

Belonging to a team channels raw talent and intelligence toward accomplishing a targeted result. Teams and departments function as singular units dedicated to accomplishing a particular piece of the company's vision. Leaders of teams and departments are responsible for keeping the vision of the company in focus and making sure that everyone on their team grasps their larger purpose within the organization.

Work Worth Doing

Communicating the company's vision to the entire organization is a tall order. How is this done? It would be nice if communicating vision in your company were as easy as printing the vision statement on a poster and sticking it up in all the break rooms. Sure, a significant first step is to get that vision for your company down on paper. But cultivating personal pride among employees for their work in your company requires much more than a poster. Personal pride in the vision and mission of an organization requires an investment of energy.

Once the vision statement is written and made known, you must ask yourself, "Do the employees know what it means? Do they feel its worth?"

Your employees must know why their work is worth doing.

"Whatever is worth doing at all is worth doing well," says the classic truism attributed to Philip Stanhope, the fourth Earl of Chesterfield.[13] "Do your work well" is usually the emphasis when this motivational quote is invoked. But the first part of the statement is just as important: "Whatever is worth doing..." This is an excellent point to consider: Why is this work worth doing? It is essential to know the answer to this.

Knowing the work is worth doing gives your employees a framework for understanding the value of their particular role in the product or service your company provides. The more employees understand the essential nature of their contributions, the more committed they are to it.

All work is routine at times, and even noble and worthy tasks have boring, mundane aspects to them. We all know the negative feeling of working at routine tasks when the work seems meaningless. Such work may be tolerable, but it does not demand our best. On the other hand, we also know the satisfaction of completing even the smallest, most mundane task when it contributes to a cause that is near to our heart. If we believe deeply in a vision, the quality of our work exceeds expectations; we innovate, improve the process, and create stunning results.

Connect the passion of purpose to your employees' work.

There is much to be gained from connecting the passion of purpose to your employees' work. Why not invest in providing opportunities that enable employees to connect the vision of your company to their sense of pride?

There is nothing more powerful than letting your employees witness the company's product having a direct impact on the community it serves. Some of your people see this every day, such as a salesperson who visits with end users about their satisfaction with the product or an engineer who conducts qualitative research to test the effectiveness of a new design. But most employees will not experience the end use of the product to which they contributed.

Change this.

Find methods and create opportunities for employees to see their work in action. The importance of this cannot be overstated.

When Pitsco can't provide direct exposure to the result for our employees, we bring the stories back to them. Through our newsletters, magazine, monthly birthday parties, and presentations at all-employee meetings, we drive home the message: who they are and what they do matters.

Ownership and Action

It's important to communicate the worthiness of your work. But another component is just as important: a system that gives employees the tools to take responsibility for that work and make it happen. No matter how strongly someone believes in a cause, if they can't make it happen, they will feel powerless and frustrated. The HOT Plan provides the system.

The answers to the following five ownership questions are crucial to every member of your team:

1. Can I bring my creativity and individuality to bear on the enterprise, or am I just here to fill a slot in an established process?
2. Does it matter what unique gifts I bring to the company, or am I just putting round pegs in round holes?
3. Am I allowed to innovate and to think for myself about how to improve the processes of my job?
4. Can I collaborate at will with others in the organization?
5. Do I have the power to make the work here my own?

*It takes a system to
convert vision to action.*

It is important to note here that empowering employees to take responsibility, innovate, and contribute to the vision is not the same thing as giving away the control of the company. In the first few years of the HOT Plan, I talked about transferring the "locus of control" instead of the "locus of responsibility" but decided later that this terminology wasn't quite right. In any organization, not everyone has equal amounts of control, but everyone needs to be given the locus of responsibility to contribute to the company's success. In the HOT Plan, success rests with employees working through their HOT Teams.

The HOT Plan moves the locus of responsibility for individual results to every employee within the company. Team members write the HOTs that put the company on course to fulfill its vision.

Departments and teams receive information about the company's Must Win Challenges (MWCs) (Chapter 6). Then, each team creates and follows their own HOTs to success. Teams write their own targets – the HOTs (Chapter 8) – not just a few here and there, but targets that cover the full range of the work, from the mundane, routine tasks to daring and explorative goals that shatter the confines of their job descriptions. As you'll learn, this method for setting goals is a core element of the HOT Plan.

You chose the best employees – now trust them.

Giving employees the power to create their own targets and pursue them requires the leadership team to define company priorities and then move out of the way. This sometimes means letting members of your organization make decisions differently than you would or take risks. It may even necessitate letting them try ideas that you are skeptical about. But you chose the best employees – now trust them. Give them space to use their intelligence and skill to build your company.

When employees are allowed to test ideas, they will learn that the power to hit or miss their targets truly rests with them. Creating a safe environment for employees to grow by learning from their mistakes will transform your culture.

The trip to St. Louis involved a second story line for Pitsco – a challenge that had a high risk of failure. Just two weeks before Pitsco employees took that bus trip, Paul, head of our Research and Development Department (R&D), was approached with an audacious idea. The Black Eyed Peas, the hip-hop band featured at the *FIRST* Championship, liked our metal-frame robotics building system so much that they asked if we could build a humanoid robot from TETRIX components that would interact with them onstage at the awards ceremony.

For those readers without an engineering background, let me tell you what Paul grasped immediately: two weeks is a harrowingly small amount of time for such an undertaking. This event was going to have national media exposure, and a robotic screwup could be very embarrassing. The project was risky and requested on very short notice, and Paul didn't have to say yes.

Something in Paul was thrilled by the challenge, and the Pitsco culture encourages reaching above-and-beyond the ordinary when the opportunity presents itself. Paul agreed to risk it. He was a madman at work for the next two weeks, still perfecting the programming of the robot in the backseat while a colleague drove him to St. Louis two days ahead of the event.

The HOT Plan's power lies in its system and in its communication.

The result was worth it. When the life-size "Mr. Robot" rolled out on his metal treads, took center stage, and raised his robotic arm in a greeting to thousands of cheering kids, Paul's work was well rewarded. We soon began getting orders for Mr. Robot kits and eventually added him to our catalog. If Paul and his R&D Team had not felt empowered to take such a risk, Pitsco would have missed out on a huge success.

Fresh Fire

The HOT Plan brings fresh fire to your business or organization by reigniting your employees' excitement for the result of their work, but communication fans the flames. The door to a highly engaged culture of success will not open wide unless the leadership talks about it all the time. The leadership must intentionally identify the vision and the MWCs and must also communicate them over and over for the HOT Plan to thrive.

Finally, *never underestimate the importance of encouragement and appreciation.* Encouragement is the spark that sets an employee's zeal on fire. Consistently tell employees that you value their innovation, personal pride, and rigor as they accomplish their targets. Risk taking pushes employees out of their comfort zone. Unless they are frequently encouraged, members of your team will tend to pull back, unsure of themselves in these uncharted territories. The word *encourage* literally means "to make strong by putting in courage."[14] Strengthen your employees with encouraging words every day.

> *Never underestimate the importance of encouragement and appreciation.*

The HOT Plan is designed to build courage in your employees. The structure of HOTs and HOT Teams provides a system to strengthen communication and pave the way for a highly engaged culture. A culture of encouragement increases employee creativity, talent, and intelligence – foundational ingredients for your organization's long-term success.

Chapter Four

The HOT Plan

So what exactly is the HOT Plan, and how did we launch it from a simple idea to the corporate workplace?

When faced with the need to rapidly reset the employee culture of Pitsco, I knew we did not have the luxury of starting from scratch or dismantling the company's structure for a do-over. Whatever system we came up with had to work within the traditional company structure that already existed.

For help with how to structure and implement the plan, I turned to Lisa, who was then our company's vice president. Lisa is gifted in many ways, but one of her greatest strengths is the ability to create systems and processes that facilitate workflow in organizations.

"I want employees to be responsible for their own jobs and for the success of the company to rest on every employee – not on the CEO or leadership team," I told Lisa. "Everyone needs to be actively involved."

The success of the company must rest on every employee.

Lisa went to work on the idea, and soon we hammered out the basics of the program. We continued to put meat on the bones of it while on business trips and in daily discussions. We talked about the importance of writing SMART goals (specific, measurable, attainable, realistic, and timely) that were more like targets than goals. Soon the title of the system fell into place. We never dreamed it would go beyond the walls of our company, so we named it something playful, something designed to bring an inside company smile. The HOT Plan was based on an acronym that originally stood for "Harvey's Official Targets." The name stood on its own, however, because everyone thought it was a truly HOT idea. The plan was HOT indeed; it fired up our company with fresh enthusiasm and provided hope that we could find our way back to an exciting and productive culture.

We implemented the program in January of the following year and in short order began to see its positive potential. During the HOT Plan's second year, there was greater clarity in our employees' understanding of how HOT Targets (HOTs) worked to their benefit. By the third year, the targets our employees created had quadrupled in number. Employees attained 83 percent of possible HOTs that year, up from 53 percent of possible targets the first year. In just three years, the HOT Plan had turned our culture around.

Today, because of the HOT Plan, Pitsco employees are highly engaged. Every team in every department creates targets. Every time a team hits their HOT Target on time, the entire company moves closer to accomplishing the Must Win Challenges (MWCs) and Key Initiatives (KIs) for the year.

Tim, Colorado-based education relationships manager and veteran Pitsco employee, shared with me the impact he saw the HOT Plan have on the internal unity of the company.

"Before the HOT Plan, our department was pretty much on an island of its own, as were other specialized departments," Tim said. "I think HOT Targets have brought us together. Everyone's HOT Targets are posted online. We can see how every department pushes the company forward."

The impact of these changes has been extraordinary. Employees at Pitsco know that every target matters, that what they contribute makes a difference. The transparency of targets and the open record of whether targets are hit or missed activate the competitive side of some teams.

Mark, another veteran employee, summarized the plan more bluntly when I asked for his thoughts.

"If you fail, everyone knows it," he said.

Because of that, Mark believes the HOTs have a grounding effect on expectations.

"When you create your HOT Targets, you tend to tie them to reality, not pie in the sky," he explained. "No team wants to be seen missing a target and the points that go with it, so you keep them attainable."

When I reached out to Suny, educational services manager who is based in another state, she said she felt the HOTs increased each employee's sense of value.

> *"[The HOT Plan] really pulls us together as a company."*
> *– Suny, educational services manager*

"It relates every employee to the company's goals," she explained. "It really pulls us together as a company. As you look at the HOT Targets, every person's contribution is significant."

Visitors notice this when they tour the campus, which happens often. Almost all of them comment on how happy our employees seem to be. It is clearly striking. Our employees today enjoy a sense of ownership in the company's progress and know that their personal contributions make a difference. I'm convinced the foundation for our employees' happiness at work comes from the HOT Plan.

The HOT Plan Defined

The HOT Plan is a team-based protocol for accomplishing targeted outcomes. In the HOT Plan, executive leadership clarifies the company vision by creating annual MWCs and KIs. Departments, teams, and employees translate these company-wide challenges and initiatives into HOTs – action-based SMART goals written with the precision of a target. Goals written with the precision of targets clearly identify **who** is going to do **what** by **when** and **what evidence (or benchmark)** will indicate that the HOT has been completed.

The leadership team approves HOTs and assigns point values. HOTs that are completed on time capture these points for a company-wide bonus pool, which accumulates over a 12-month period. The captured points are assigned a dollar value at the end of the year and culminate in an equally shared reward bonus – the HOT Check – that we give to all employees in January.

The HOT Check is not a traditional profit- or stock-sharing plan. Team leaders assign due dates for HOTs and point values based on the time they anticipate it will take to complete the HOTs. There is complete transparency in point totals. Each time a team completes a HOT Target on time, points are captured for the bonus total. Leadership reports points via *HOTware*™, a database on the company intranet, as well as the company newsletter.

The HOT Plan can be adapted to many different organizations, but certain fundamentals are necessary to make sure it succeeds. Following is a brief overview of these.

HOT Plan Fundamentals

1. Establish working teams to address the company's strategic goals.

First, establish the leadership team. The leadership team should be made up of executive leaders and the heads of departments. The task of this team is to develop the broad strategy for the organization. At Pitsco, this team is called Tribal Council and sets our company's direction by creating an annual list of three to five MWCs and as many KIs as necessary to carry them out (Chapter 6).

Tribal Council creates other functional teams for specific, ongoing purposes in accomplishing the company vision (Chapter 14). The council chooses team members for their expertise in diverse areas of the company, across department lines, and for the specific skills they contribute. Departments also function as their own HOT Teams.

2. Teams write HOTs.

Teams write HOTs to correlate with the MWCs and KIs established by the leadership team. In addition, HOTs encompass day-to-day tasks, cultural goals, above-and-beyond opportunities, and even open targets for unexpected projects that arise throughout the year (Chapter 8).

3. The leadership team reviews the targets to ensure a sound, big-picture plan.

The HOT Plan Champion and key leadership read and evaluate submitted targets for relevance to the MWCs and KIs. After evaluating the targets, leadership recommends them for acceptance or notes of concern. If there are concerns, the HOTs are sent back to the team to revise and resubmit.

4. Assign HOTs a point value and a due date.

The leadership team assigns the point values associated with approved targets. Point values are based on the estimated amount of work time needed to complete the target. Point values provide an objective measurement by which overall progress toward accomplishing HOTs can be tracked and by which the cash bonus can later be calculated (Chapter 8).

5. Each team meets regularly.

Teams discuss their overall progress in meeting HOTs regularly. Each team has a recorder who plays a critical role in writing accurate minutes and submitting them to the leadership team. Minutes include updates on progress and plans being made toward the completion of targets (Chapter 7).

6. Point gains and losses are continually updated.

As mentioned earlier, point gains and losses are posted via the company intranet, monthly employee meetings, and the company newsletter. Transparency is a vital part of the system.

7. A dollar multiplier for points earned is assigned at year's end.

A final accounting at the end of the year will determine the bonus payable to every employee. The final accounting is a summation of the total points all teams earn during the year, multiplied by a fixed dollar amount the leadership team determines at the year-end. The resulting sum of money is divided equally among employees and presented as a bonus check known as the HOT Check (Chapters 5, 8).

If you've read this far, I know you are looking for a solution for your company, classroom, team, or organization. We have spent close to 20 years tweaking the HOT Plan, and we know that if you give it a chance, it will work for you. In the coming chapters, we hope to spell out the plan in such a way that you can get started right away. For reference, here are the questions we will answer in the chapters ahead:

- How do you write HOTs? (Chapter 8)
- How do HOTs connect to the MWCs and KIs? (Chapter 8)
- How are deadlines and points determined? (Chapters 8, 10)
- How do groups know when their HOTs have been completed? (Chapter 8)
- How does the program promote employee growth and creativity? (Chapters 8, 9)
- How does work flow through the organization? (Chapters 6, 7, 10, 11, 12)
- How is the progress of each group tracked? (Chapters 6, 8, 9)
- How are changes integrated into the work plan? (Chapter 8)
- How is transparency maintained? (Chapters 6, 7)
- How is progress maintained? (Chapters 7, 10, 11, 12)
- How are successes celebrated? (Chapters 5, 7)

Reflections

Including employees in the target-setting process and giving them the resources and freedom to accomplish the HOTs as well as a share in the rewards of that accomplishment, moves the locus of responsibility for the company's success to the employee where it belongs. The HOT Plan enables employees to own and be responsible for their segment of the work needed to fulfill the company vision.

Putting the locus of responsibility in the hands of employees positions them to be leaders. When an entire cadre of leaders puts their energy, passion, and ideas behind your vision, it's an exciting experience. But as an owner-entrepreneur with strong opinions of my own, this requires something from me. I have to be willing to listen to my employees, to allow their input, and even at times to let go of my preconceived ideas of how things should be done. Since the company has grown, I no longer know all of my employees as well as I did in the past, but I still must extend my trust to them for the HOT Plan to work. To trust is not always easy, because to trust is to risk.

To trust is not easy, because to trust is to risk.

In our case the risk paid off. We've seen an increase in effectiveness since instituting the HOT Plan in 1997. The plan produced greater clarity of direction and improved our profitability and culture. The individual roles of employees and teams are more clearly defined. Our bottom line has steadily improved. Pitsco's company-wide success in hitting HOTs increased from 53 percent the first year to a high of 92 percent and then settled to a steady 88 percent for many years.

Today, because of the HOT Plan, I am no longer at the center of the web. Teams and departments are deeply networked within the company and have a high degree of autonomy. They collaborate easily. Some of my lifelong ideals for the workplace are flourishing before my eyes. It is good to have an ideal in mind for your workplace, but unless you have a reliable method for putting that ideal into practice, it will never become a reality.

Do the ideals for the workplace I've described in this book appeal to you? Are you ready to take your organization to the next level? If so, then the HOT Plan may be for you.

In fact, I would like to make a pledge to you.

In the following pages, I will show you how to make the HOT Plan work. I will explain the thinking behind its many facets and the structures for its success and even throw in a few things we have learned along the way that will shorten your timeline to success.

For us, the HOT Plan has become more than just a company incentive program; it is the foundation of our highly engaged culture. The HOT Plan is our accountability program, the basis of employee evaluation, an incentive program, a structure defining the flow of work in our organization, a system of communication between areas of the company, and a tool for encouraging innovation and buy-in among employees.

The HOT Plan is the basis of our culture.

The HOT Plan turned our company around, and it can do the same for you. But before we dive into the details, we must explore one more secret to success.

Chapter Five

Success Shared

Each January, with the holidays just behind us, we schedule a New Year's celebration to go over the numbers of the past year's accomplishments and pass out nearly 200 hot checks.

Yes, we admit it. We give out hot checks. And in fact, we love doing it. These checks are not hot because of insufficient funds in the company bank account; rather, they are HOT because they are the HOT Plan's method of sharing success.

Success is earned in common; therefore, success is shared in common.

Any bonus is exciting, of course; even the first-year $92 HOT Check was extra money in the employees' pockets, and that felt good just after Christmas. But at that moment I dreamed of the day that a HOT Check could be $1,000 or more. To my satisfaction, the amount has grown steadily and several years ago it reached the $1,000 mark. Then HOT Teams worked company-wide to push the amount even higher. The most recent checks have surpassed $1,800.

The exact amount of the HOT Check comes with an element of surprise. Employees crowd into our campus café with excitement and the camaraderie that comes from a shared accomplishment. Lisa, the company president, leads an annual report presentation and invites me to speak. I always thank employees for their work, reminding them of our vision: *leading education that positively affects learners*. Other employees contribute to the annual report, and Lisa compares the number of HOT Points from prior years to the number possible in the new year.

An excitement ripples across the room when she finally announces the dollar amount of the year's HOT Check. Checks are prepared before the meeting so that employees can pick them up as they leave. This ritual transforms the meeting from an annual obligation to an annual anticipation.

In recent years, we have added a perk – one that some employees have touted as their favorite part. Teams that achieve 100 percent of their targets are entered in a drawing to receive an additional HOT

Check as a team. But this HOT Check is to give away. I draw five teams from the pool. Each of these five teams chooses a charity, a program, or any group they wish to support with the extra HOT Check. We report the recipients of their contributions in our company newsletter.

Celeste, senior project manager from Spartanburg, South Carolina, shared with me that donating the gift to charity was her favorite part. Her whole team submitted ideas as to how it should be spent.

"In the end, we voted to help kids at risk as dropouts by donating to a Star Academy," she shared. "Everyone was excited about making a difference for these kids; it was very meaningful to all of us."

The Power of Rewards

People outside of Pitsco sometimes raise an eyebrow when they hear about the HOT Check. They question the idea of tying HOT Targets (HOTs) to a monetary reward. But it is the financial incentive that keeps the HOTs grounded, said Mark, teacher education specialist.

"Incentivizing the HOT Plan ... forces the conversation to become more realistic."
– Mark, teacher education specialist

Mark remembers that Pitsco always had annual goals. But for him, the HOT Plan brought those goals into focus by converting them to targets with a financial incentive. As he sees it, the HOT Check provides positive pressure and serves as a grounding force in the goal-setting process.

"Incentivizing the HOT Plan has power because it forces the conversation to become more realistic. People are less likely to throw something out there that is overly idealistic," Mark explained. "If someone presents a target, the question will be asked: Realistically, do we have a shot of pulling that off?"

Suny, educational services manager from South Carolina, sees the financial incentive as team building.

Shared rewards are a team-building initiative.

"The money piece is interesting," she said. "It contributes to the sense that we are all in this together; it is a team-building initiative."

Beyond team building, the HOT Check represents a type of reward that millennials seek. Millennials surveyed for the PwC study (Chapter 2) said the creation of a "meaningful rewards structure that regularly acknowledges both large and small contributions made by employees" is critical to them in choosing an employer.[15]

Why Are HOT Checks Equal?

A second eyebrow-raiser for some people is the idea of giving equal reward checks to all employees, regardless of their rank in the company.

In many compensation plans, bonus checks vary in amount according to the rank or seniority of employees; the higher the corporate ranking or the greater the seniority, the bigger the bonus check. The idea behind scaled bonus amounts is motivation. In other words, loyalty, perseverance, and sometimes even political maneuvering are rewarded if employees can weather the demands with long-term perks in view. From the perspective of that tradition, the HOT Plan's approach of distributing rewards equally to all employees through HOT Checks flies in the face of logic.

The truth is that the HOT Check reward is consistent with a different type of logic; a logic that is team based. According to the HOT Plan, success is the result of a team effort. Therefore, if a company succeeds, it is because every employee contributed a vital part.

> *Success is earned in common; therefore, it should be shared in common.*

Are there some employees who walk out with a full HOT Check but did not do their fair share to earn it? Perhaps. That possibility always exists. There may be a few in our company who aren't doing their fair share, but honestly, if this is the case, I don't know them. The better we have become at sharing the locus of responsibility with our employees over the years, the more committed our employees have become to giving their best efforts to accomplish the HOTs.

A word here seems necessary to address other types of company bonuses. In any company with an active sales force, there are many other types of incentives, commissions, and sales-based bonuses. The HOT Check does not replace these. The HOT Check reward is restricted to the amount earned annually by the collective efforts of all departments and teams as they successfully hit their HOTs.

Equality Fosters Leadership

Equal bonus checks communicate that the work of all employees is equally valuable to your company's success. The positive impact of this cannot be overstated; equality cultivates a culture of leadership.

Employees take responsibility for meeting their own HOTs, but in order to sustain their enthusiasm throughout the year for the company's progress, it is crucial that they see how their work affects the whole company. Points posted online motivate teams; they can see when they are doing well or when they need to push a little harder. *HOTware*™ shows when targets are accomplished and when they are missed; it also shows the points adding up. Tracking the targets provides the additional benefit of communicating the overall company progress as the year moves along.

Equality of value cultivates a culture of leadership.

Dorcia, senior development specialist and project manager, uses the HOT Plan as a way to transfer accountability directly to our employees. Dorcia shared with me that because the plan is easily understood by employees, it is therefore easily followed.

"We all understand that each goal has a point value and that each point value has a corresponding dollar value," she said. "Literally, each goal we complete is money in our pockets."

David, curriculum specialist, said his experiences with goal setting and accomplishments in other workplaces were not always positive. He compared past experiences to the old carrot-and-stick motivational strategy.

"Most places have goals that are like a stick without a carrot," he shared. "Each missed goal adds weight to that stick, which is used to beat you at the end of the year during your evaluation."

But to David, the HOT Plan uses the carrot, not the stick, to motivate employees. HOTs and HOT Points keep the reward in view.

"Reaching targets not only offers a real carrot, but waters it and makes it grow. When you finally get to have the carrot at HOT Check time, it's bigger and sweeter," David explained. "The HOT Targets put the emphasis on accomplishment."

The ability to look forward to the targeted goals ahead and to look back at what has already been achieved is a vital skill for leaders. This ability gives employees a practical awareness of the company's progress toward accomplishing the Must Win Challenges (MWCs) for the year and helps keep long-term projects in sight. HOTs provide bite-size, intermittent deadlines that help accomplish the annual MWCs and Key Initiatives (KIs).

The HOT Plan puts the emphasis on accomplishment.

In track and field, we called short-term running targets "five-minute goals." These were especially useful when you wanted to quit exercising. You could almost always convince yourself to push for just five more minutes. Then, when that five-minute mark arrived, it seemed so much easier to do just five minutes more. In a similar way, targets give a string of approaching deadlines that pace the work of the HOT Plan in incremental performance pushes.

Rewarding Relationships

The phrase "our Pitsco family" is used commonly on campus. We not only work together, we also laugh together, pray together, share food at potluck birthday parties together, contribute to causes together, and, when necessary, mourn together. Employees frequently cite the family culture as their favorite aspect of working for the company. In the most obvious sense, the phrase "our Pitsco family" indicates the wholesomeness of Pitsco's workplace culture, but it also refers to something deeper – a bond among employees that goes beyond the workplace.

Before our company president Lisa worked for us, she worked for a large corporation. At that company, she was one of 17,000 employees. The company based its bonuses on individual rank and accomplishment instead of on collective achievements. To Lisa, the two systems produce radically different cultures. The traditional business bonus structure fosters individualism, while the HOT Plan fosters teamwork and close-knit, team-based relationships.

"The difference is refreshing," Lisa said.

No doubt the people she worked with at the other company were also good, hardworking, and considerate people. But the goal-setting system of the company was typical – built on individuals looking out for themselves in order to get ahead – and just as predictably, produced a less relational culture.

The HOTs leverage the power of community rather than individualism in your workplace. As most of us have experienced, accountability to and for others produces a deep level of motivation in us. Not only does accountability to others motivate us, but a sense of our own importance and responsibility for our team's success brings out the best in us. So why not tap into these natural tendencies at work?

> *HOT Targets leverage the power of community.*

Tom, communications manager, confided in me that he wasn't sold on the HOT Plan right away.

"I wondered if it might just be a contrived effort to get employees to do what they should already be doing," he shared. "Over time, though, I came to realize it's a win-win-win for the company, employees, and customers. Everyone benefits when HOTs are achieved."

Fostering Trust

Trust is a baseline for a healthy culture.

The HOT Plan trusts employees to enhance the amount of their HOT Check by submitting and accomplishing as many points as they believe they can achieve through their teams and departments.

In visiting with business leaders throughout the years, I've learned some companies do not like to entrust this kind of responsibility to their employees. They fear employees will take advantage of the system and use it for personal gain. In nearly 20 years, however, we've never had this problem.

Trust is a baseline for a healthy culture.

The HOT Plan was created with internal checks and balances to prevent abuse. Checks and balances include caveats such as approval for all HOTs and reduced points for late targets. But beyond the system's internal checks and balances, trust is at the root of the HOT Plan.

Our Tribal Council encourages the Pitsco teams to earn as many HOT Points as possible each year. This can get expensive for the company. For example, there were 3,640 points possible in 2008. Just one year later, there were 5,159 points possible – a startling amount of growth. But no matter how high the possible points climb, we always hope that our employees will hit 100 percent of their targets. Hitting targets is in everyone's best interest.

The Reward of Success

From my perspective, the HOT Point total gives a quantitative value to those aspects of business that are difficult to measure. We can measure profitability in product sales and dollar amounts or increases in our company's annual bottom line. But how do we measure the success of our culture?

The growing number of HOTs and the increased number of points attained by our teams form a metric by which to measure our thriving business culture.

The HOT Check helps employees keep the goal in view.

It didn't take long to discover that the HOT Check reward was more than a nice gesture – it was an essential part of the plan. The HOT Check keeps the goal in view. The power that teams have to increase their annual bonus checks by gaining HOT Points helps to keep the HOTs challenging – and authentic.

To be completely transparent, our first few years with the HOT Plan were challenging at times. Getting it right didn't happen overnight. Some of the staff were skeptical at first; others assumed the HOT Plan was just another idea that would make more work for everyone and then blow over. But in sticking with the HOT Plan over the years and working through the challenges, employees saw the lasting value of the program and embraced it.

So there you have it – the story of the HOT Plan and how it grew from a plan to save a high school track team in one of the poorest counties of Oklahoma to a successful corporate solution for employee engagement and millennial workforce changes in the early 21st century. Naturally, there's a lot more to learn if you want to make the HOT Plan a part of your story. But if you've read this far and are feeling the itch to see how the HOT Plan might work for the success of your organization, then the rest of this book is for you.

Part II. HOT Fundamentals

Chapters

6. HOT Evolution

7. HOT Teams

8. HOT Targets

9. HOT Accountability

Chapter Six

HOT Evolution

Moving beyond the beginnings of a new idea is a challenging phase. Entering this phase is a good sign because it means that your idea is growing; things are alive and moving in a positive direction. But getting past the basics can launch you into some perilous waters.

We developed the HOT Plan because our organization stalled and we needed to get things back on track. Health in an organization, just like in an individual, is the foundation for everything else.

Good organizational health leads to profitability. Healthy organizations "align, execute, and renew [themselves] faster than the competition" and are able to sustain exceptional performance over time, according to Scott Keller and Colin Price in their book *Beyond Performance*.[16]

To Patrick Lencioni, business consultant and author, strong organizational health is a sign of integrity, the type of integrity that comes from consistency.

"A [healthy] organization has [organizational] integrity ..." Lencioni says in his book *The Advantage*. Integrity in this sense means seamless integration: when the organization's "management, operations, strategy, and culture fit together and make sense."[17]

> *Getting smarter together also means a commitment to learning as a team.*

Healthy organizations even make their members "smarter," he says. This is partially because healthy organizations cultivate the process of learning from their mistakes and employees are encouraged to learn from each other, together figuring out ways to recover quickly from their missteps. Office politics are minimized by a company-wide focus on the endgame, and mistakes are accepted as an inevitable part of the journey.

Conversely, if you lose your health, the quest for recovery takes over and everything grinds to a halt.

When we lost our organizational health, we found our recovery in the HOT Plan. It got us started again, gave the energy back, helped teamwork thrive, and restored high morale. The HOT Plan not only helped us regain our health but also gave us the tools to stay strong in the years ahead.

In this chapter, we share the evolution of the HOT Plan: our journey along the learning curve and what it looks like today. We also answer some frequently asked questions about how to make it work for you.

Our HOT Plan Learning Curve

"The HOT Plan has evolved," said Pitsco President Lisa. "The core of the HOT Plan has been the same since 1997 when it was first conceived, but the things we have done to make it stronger and easier to administrate have developed over time."

So how steep was our own learning curve with the HOT Plan? Well, you might say that when we began this program, we had nowhere to go but up.

When Lisa came to our company as assistant chief financial officer, she noticed that, like many successful entrepreneurial businesses, the business processes were driven by demand rather than protocol. Solutions were worked out mostly as needed instead of through systems. As an accountant, Lisa immediately saw a need to define systems and processes.

When I shared with her the basic idea of the HOT Plan, she saw potential for developing business process routines. She set out to establish the systems needed to support the HOT Plan's success. She started by helping to create guidelines for how teams would be set up, the processes by which people would submit and record points, and how the annual bonus amount would be determined.

"When we first started," Lisa recalled, "HOTs were submitted on paper. We used SMART goals as the benchmark for HOT Targets. We read all of them and assigned the point values loosely based on how much work each target required. There was no flexibility; either you made the deadline and got the points, or you missed the deadline and missed the points. But after the first two years, we became more flexible."

We became more flexible because we learned two things: 1) it's surprisingly hard for most people to write goals, and 2) it gets even harder when more than one person is involved. And when the fulfillment of HOT Targets (HOTs) involved the coordination of more than one team or department, meeting a deadline could be tricky.

It is surprisingly hard for most people to write effective goals.

"We soon learned to catch HOTs in the planning stages," Lisa said. "If more than one department must coordinate in order to complete a target, we now ask all departments involved to work out the timing and scheduling of shared HOTs in advance, before the HOTs are submitted for approval."

We also added a process for extending deadlines for delayed HOTs if circumstances warranted.

"At first, our HOTs were not aligned with overarching company objectives. But after the first couple of years, we saw a need to tie the HOT Targets to the big picture," Lisa said. "Our first company-wide target was cost savings and our second was student success."

Adding the two overarching targets laid the groundwork for the system we use today, guided by the annually updated Must Win Challenges (MWCs) and Key Initiatives (KIs).

Over time, different types of HOTs began to multiply. We found it necessary to add categories. Today, we have four types of HOTs: Operational HOTs, Above-and-Beyond HOTs, Cultural HOTs, and Open HOTs. Teams write HOTs in each category.

As the types of HOTs multiplied, assigning points proved to be more difficult. Previously, this was done by the HOT Champion, but eventually the process had to be standardized. Today, all teams use a chart that sets the points according to the hours estimated to complete each HOT. Teams estimate the time and points required, and therefore the points to be awarded, before they submit their HOTs for approval.

> *The HOT Plan can help you successfully navigate times of enormous change.*

All of these changes were a part of our journey on the learning curve. We constantly asked ourselves how we could help the HOT Plan operate more smoothly. We discovered it is important to relax and experiment with fitting the HOT Plan to the company's needs, and these needs change with time. You, too, must adapt the HOT Plan to fit your needs. Maximizing the HOT Plan's effectiveness, however, requires that you stick to the values underlying the HOT Plan, its basic philosophies, and its proven structure.

Second-Generation HOT Plan

The HOT Plan has successfully carried our company through enormous change. Recently, when a major division of our operations was divested from Pitsco, Tribal Council used the HOT Plan to navigate the transition.

The change introduced uncertainty for Pitsco employees – an uncertainty that had negative potential. However, Matt, our vice president of education, viewed the change positively; he saw it as an opportunity to reenergize the HOT Plan and make it more tightly focused on the company's future. He credits a snowstorm and a canceled flight for the discovery of the key to refining the HOT Plan in the midst of Pitsco's transition.

"I ended up stranded in Atlanta due to a snowstorm that shut down my destination airport," Matt said. "So I decided to kill some of that time at a Barnes and Noble bookstore. It was there that I noticed a book called *The Advantage* by Patrick Lencioni. When I saw the subtitle, 'Why Organizational Health Trumps Everything Else in Business,' I immediately connected with the book."

> *"If you don't have a healthy culture, you may miss the next opportunity."*
> *– Matt, vice president of education*

Matt bought *The Advantage* and was not disappointed. Lencioni's thesis is that "the single greatest advantage any company can achieve is organizational health." This idea rang true with Matt.

"If you don't have a healthy culture," Matt said, "you may miss the next opportunity."

Matt shared the book with Lisa, who also recognized the value of Lencioni's insights for navigating Pitsco's transition. They presented the book to Tribal Council as their next shared study book.

Pitsco had a healthy culture but needed to increase clarity to navigate these changes. Lencioni maps out a process for creating clarity, overcommunicating clarity, and reinforcing clarity. Using these concepts as guidelines, Tribal adapted the HOT Plan in the following ways:

- Tribal created a one-page playbook that outlines the core values and targets of the company. Leadership references this playbook when a critical decision needs to be made.
- The leadership identified and published three to five MWCs for the coming year.
- KIs were identified that aligned with the MWCs.
- The leadership nested the KIs under MWCs so that their connection to the company's strategic priorities would be absolutely clear. KIs were also published in company communications.
- The budget was aligned with the MWCs and budget updates are reported monthly.
- Employees were asked to create HOTs in line with the KIs. The relationship between the KIs and the MWCs was published both on- and offline. As a result, HOT Teams could see how their work moved the company forward.
- Tribal instituted a monthly meeting for the entire company for a progress report, awards, and recognition.

The new clarity and increased communication brought fresh energy to the company, according to Matt.

"It gave us a laser-like focus," he told me.

As a result, Matt got a great deal of positive feedback from employees.

"The beauty of it, according to the feedback I've received, has been the sharpened focus and the resulting confidence that these changes have brought to us," Matt said.

Employees said it helped them to know that their individual work was moving the company in the direction of profitability.

"Because of this connection, the individual teams and departments feel more cohesive," he said.

To Lisa, the goal of the HOT Plan changes is simple: continuous improvement.

"We will always be growing and refining," Lisa said. "It doesn't behoove us to stop changing."

How It Looks Today

As you can see, the HOT Plan we use at Pitsco today is a refined system that required years of tweaking and improving. From the plan's small beginnings – a few cross-disciplinary HOT Teams – to today's integration of HOTs at all levels, we have continued to find ways to increase the HOT Plan's impact and efficiency.

As we have said before, the HOT Targets today have become a part of the very ethos of our company culture. We use them to facilitate activities and workflow and also to support our overarching initiatives.

The foundation of the HOT Plan at Pitsco is our vision statement: *leading education that positively affects learners.* This is our commitment to action, not an adage to frame and hang on the boardroom wall. Pitsco's vision statement is a living bedrock upon which everything else in the company is built.

Pitsco's Four Brand Pillars (core competencies) are rock-solid commitments to quality. They rest upon our vision statement: Student Success Through Engagement, Purpose Driven to Make a Difference, Industry-Leading Customer Service, and Quality/Innovative Curriculum and Products. Like the foundation, these competencies hold firm, providing steady support for the company's products and services regardless of market demands.

The vision statement provides a bedrock upon which everything else is built.

Resting upon these pillars are our annual MWCs, KIs, and HOTs for the year. Tribal Council updates them annually to align Pitsco with the current education market. We develop new products and update old favorites as necessary to keep up with the changes in technology and current education standards.

This process is founded on input from every area of the company. The first step of the process is defining the big picture. This definition begins with the development of three to five MWCs that articulate the focus of the coming year. MWCs are large, overarching statements that guide the direction of the company. An example of an MWC is "Increase revenue and profitability."

After identifying three to five MWCs, Tribal writes Key Initiatives. KIs are specific projects that apply the MWCs. An example of a KI is to "Design and develop 30 new products." This aligns with the MWC "Increase revenue and profitability." Another recent KI, "Develop Math *Expeditions*," aligns with the MWC "Develop products that meet academic standards."

Next, the HOTs take center stage. These bite-size targets translate the big ideas into action. About 60 percent of all HOTs link to the KIs, while 40 percent of the HOTs link to daily operations, Cultural HOTs, or unexpected projects that arise during the year. As mentioned in Chapter 4, HOTs not only guide our work, but because they have point values, they also give us a measure of our progress throughout the year.

Linking MWCs, KIs, and HOTs gave Pitsco a tightened alignment of management, operations, strategy, and company culture at a critical time. This strengthened our organizational integrity. As Lencioni asserts, organizational integrity is at the very core of organizational health.

HOT Architecture

From the foundation up, the structure of Pitsco's HOT Plan today looks like this: (*see illustration on the next page*)

- **The Vision**

    Pitsco's vision provides a bedrock upon which everything else is built.

    "Leading education that positively affects learners."

- **The Pillars**

    The Pillars provide the foundation upon which the MWCs, KIs, and HOTs rest. Pillars are the core competencies of the company, the things we do better than everyone else. Our Pillars differentiate us from our competitors.

- **Must Win Challenges (MWCs)**

    MWCs are the issues we must face in the short term in order to be successful. They are broad and overarching. MWCs provide clarity and focus for the KIs and the HOTs.

- **Key Initiatives (KIs)**

    KIs provide the specifics of what we must accomplish to say we won the challenge. Each KI includes a description of the requirements for achieving an MWC.

- **HOT Targets (HOTs)**

    Team statements include who will accomplish the target, what will be accomplished, the date that the target will be accomplished, and how success will be benchmarked.

The HOT Plan™

TARGETS

Targets are statements that indicate who will do what, and when the target will be achieved, including evidence of completion.

1. Expand robotics portfolio
2. Develop middle school products
3. Develop elementary products
4. Improve international processes
5. Develop employees
6. Secure grants
7. Manage product lifecycles
8. Increase brand awareness
9. Maximize Big Data tools
10. Track customer metrics
11. Develop STEM competitions
12. Improve operational efficiencies
13. Increase social engagement

KEY INITIATIVES

| INCREASE REVENUE AND PROFITABILITY | DEVELOP PRODUCTS THAT MEET STANDARDS | EDUCATE INTERNAL AND EXTERNAL STAKE HOLDERS | DEVELOP METRICS TO UNDERSTAND CUSTOMER BEHAVIOR | CONNECT DATA SILOS TO CREATE OPERATIONAL DIFFERENCES |

MUST WIN CHALLENGES

| STUDENT SUCCESS THROUGH ENGAGEMENT | PURPOSE DRIVEN TO MAKE A DIFFERENCE | INDUSTRY LEADING CUSTOMER SERVICE | QUALITY/ INNOVATIVE CURRICULUM AND PRODUCTS |

CORPORATE PILLARS

"Leading education that positively affects learners!"

VISION ← Start Here

PITSCO EDUCATION

The HOT Plan™ begins with the Vision and is carried out through Targets. More than 1,400 Targets carry out the above HOT Plan.

Learning Curve

There is a learning curve when it comes to implementing any change, and the HOT Plan is no exception. Even something as positive as having more say in how things get done in the workplace is uncomfortable for some employees. Be patient if it takes a while before a true understanding of the HOT Plan filters throughout your company. If you anticipate that the learning curve for your organization will be steep, change things slowly – begin with just the bare bones of the program. As you get the hang of it, you can add more elements.

Having more say in how things get done is a new concept for some employees.

For example, when we began the HOT Plan, only the interdepartmental HOT Teams wrote targets, but regular departments did not. Consequently, a large number of employees had no involvement with writing targets. We soon found this to be limiting. We then expanded HOT Teams to include departments and asked each department to write their day-to-day goals for operations in the form of HOTs.

Including the departments as HOT Teams was the quickest way to bring everyone on board and get them involved. This single change shortened the learning curve for the HOT Plan.

Frequently Asked Questions

Here are questions we often encounter from other business leaders interested in adapting the HOT Plan themselves:

1. Who makes changes or updates to our company's HOT Plan?

Changes to the HOT Plan are decided by the executive team, the ultimate keeper of the program's policies, and are interpreted in real time by the HOT Champion.

2. How frequently should changes/updates to the program be made?

While I think it is healthy to modify the program to suit needs as they develop, I would caution organizations not to make changes frequently. It took some time at Pitsco before employees fully understood the program. Our leadership team had to demonstrate commitment to the idea before the employees bought in. If we had appeared too flighty in the rules we laid down for the process, the proving phase might have lasted longer. It certainly would have extended the learning curve.

3. How do you know when a change/update to the HOT Plan is truly necessary?

When you have made an addition or alteration, remember that you have two great metrics to help you: the number of targets submitted versus the percentage of targets completed. The number of targets submitted gives a quantitative measure of your teams' ambition, and the percentage of targets completed gives a quantitative measure of how effectively your employees are able to complete their work. If you put these two metrics together, you will see whether your HOT Plan is doing its job or needs revision.

The transparency surrounding targets and points is one of the big benefits of keeping good records of the program from year to year. Pitsco employees get excited about the prospect of topping their percentages from each previous year, thus increasing their bonus. Members of your organization will too.

4. How do you keep track of all those points?

In the beginning, we had nothing but *Excel* files and paper printouts to keep track of points. Finally, we commissioned our IT staff to develop a database tool – *HOTware*™.

The creation of *HOTware* was one of the greatest leaps forward for the HOT Plan in our company. Depending on the size of your organization, it is still possible to run a HOT Plan without a database, but we can't imagine going without the software these days.

We use *HOTware* to submit targets for approval and also to track targets as they are completed and totaled.

Moving Beyond Kansas

I am confident that the HOT Plan will continue to grow and evolve at Pitsco, and I hope that it will grow well beyond our corner of Southeast Kansas. When I created it, I did not expect it to be used by other companies and organizations. At the time, we had concerns that seemed unique. Time and experience taught me that our problems are common among growing organizations. I began to realize that the HOT Plan could help others too.

Ultimately, if you choose to implement this plan, you need to adapt it in ways that are right for you. That being said, some mechanisms of the HOT Plan can't be changed without killing the plan's spirit and effectiveness. Here are five unchangeables:

Five Unchangeables of the HOT Plan

1 The HOT Plan begins with who you are as an organization: your vision, your pillars, your MWCs, and the KIs that help you reach your goals.

2 An executive leadership team is needed to determine the big picture and communicate the overall plan.

3 Supervisors coach members of HOT Teams to successfully write and accomplish targets.

4 HOT Teams write targets and decide how to pursue them.

5 All employees are rewarded for their efforts with an equally-shared financial bonus that they have earned together.

If you do these five things with enthusiasm and diligence, the HOT Plan will work for you. Are you ready to make a positive change in your organization's health and culture? If the answer is yes, congratulations! The journey you are about to embark upon is one of the best ways to multiply productivity and increase employee satisfaction.

If you follow the five unchangeables, the HOT Plan will work for you.

Conversely, if you choose not to work toward greater organizational health, casualties can and will occur in your business culture. As Lencioni indicates, such casualties are far-reaching.

"The impact of organizational health goes far beyond the walls of a company, extending to customers and vendors, even to spouses and children," says Lencioni. "It sends people to work in the morning with clarity, hope, and anticipation and brings them home at night with a greater sense of accomplishment, contribution, and self-esteem. The impact of this is as important as it is impossible to measure."[18]

I hope the HOT Plan will be the pathway you choose to take on your journey toward greater organizational health. The key to making the HOT Plan work for you is teamwork. In the next chapter, we will get into some straightforward advice on how to set up high-performance teams. As I learned in my years coaching at Weleetka, building a high-performance team takes time, energy, and commitment. But nothing drives a company forward as powerfully as the synergy of team members working together to accomplish a common goal.

Chapter Seven

HOT Teams

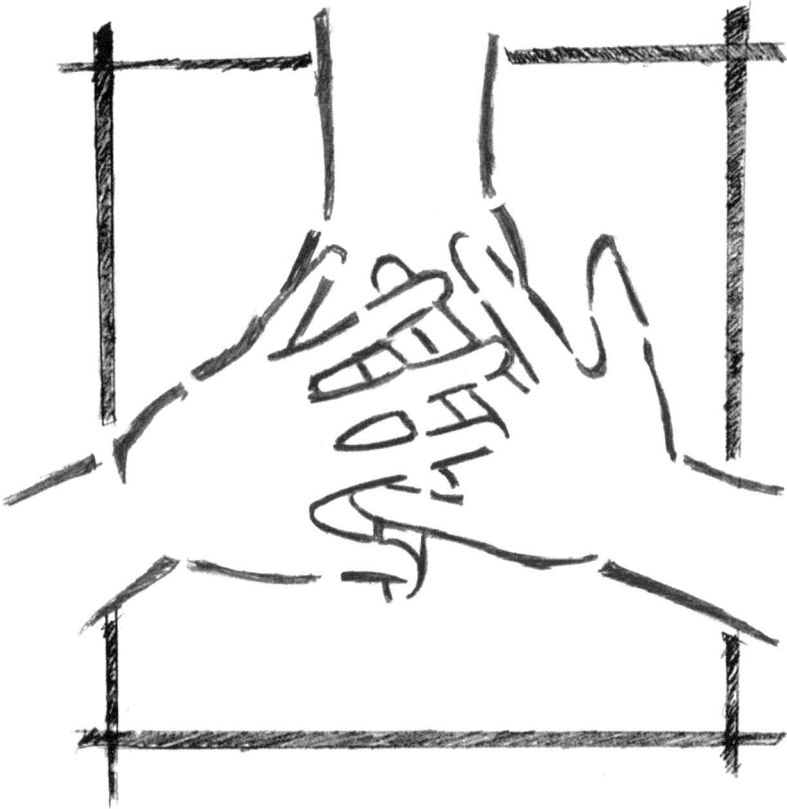

A well-assembled team is like a precision lens that magnifies the strengths of its individual members. Remember that track team I coached? In Weleetka, the boys, as individuals, had no direction, had won no awards, and had no foundation of athletic training. By combining our efforts and focusing on our shared goal of winning medals, as a team we soon became greater than the sum of our parts.

In the business world it works much the same way. Individuals flourish on teams because of a team's synergistic ability to multiply creativity, motivation, and problem-solving skills. Because of the unique strength of teams, we designed the HOT Plan as a team-based system.

In the classic book *The Wisdom of Teams* by best-selling authors Jon Katzenbach and Douglas Smith, teams are defined as "a small number of people with complementary skills who are committed to a common purpose, performance goals, and approach for which they hold themselves mutually accountable."[19]

According to Katzenbach and Smith, teams "should be the basic unit of performance for most organizations, regardless of size."[20]

To create and market products across international borders requires collaboration.

This key role for teams continues to grow. In the results of a Towers Watson global workforce study – based on interviews with more than 32,000 employees from mid- to large-size businesses across a range of industries in 29 markets – a revolution of sorts is seen to be taking place in the world of work.[21] In every market studied around the world, the image of the individualistic and self-sufficient "worker bee" is increasingly losing its currency as a metaphor for the modern employee.

Instead, the collaborative team member is taking its place. Almost half of those interviewed reported working "remotely or in some kind of flexible arrangement." Jobs that were once carried out from start to finish in one geographic locale are now being broken into components, reorganized, and dispersed across teams in different time zones.

Driving the teamwork trend is the increasingly specialized knowledge of the global marketplace. To create and market products across international borders requires collaboration. Ironically, as the markets become more global, demands increase for more individual attention. Only teams can keep up with those demands. The ability to work on high-performance teams is a necessity in today's business world.

The Magic of Teams

Teams in business are often drawn from different departments and thus have greater agility than the individual departments they represent. This is because the team brings together a company-wide perspective and provides a well-rounded approach. Initially, all HOT Targets were written by this type of interdepartmental HOT Teams. Later, departments became HOT Teams as well. Interdepartmental teams remain the backbone of the HOT Plan, however. Why?

HOT Teams have greater agility than individual departments.

Interdepartmental teams have a knack for getting at those places that traditional hierarchies find difficult to reach. When Pitsco launched the TETRIX® robotics product line, for example, we created an interdepartmental HOT Team to sustain the product launch over a three- to four-year period. The team had the ability to coordinate various departments in great precision because of their cross connections. This was critical to the success of the launch.

"When we created a robotics team to introduce the new product line, we knew it was going to be a long-term team," recalled Lisa, our president. "Robotics education is very hot, and TETRIX is at the leading edge of our product line. We needed complete cooperation across the company to launch this with maximum effectiveness."

The TETRIX PRIME launch team consisted of representatives from each part of the company, including the research and development manager, the robotics product specialist, a curriculum specialist manager, the marketing director, the international sales director, and the web director, as well as a representative from compliance and the physical plant operations director. For the first year, the TETRIX launch team met every two weeks. Frequency of communication – both face to face and electronic – was critical.

Coordinating a product launch is a classic example of the criticality of a team, especially when a launch is international.

But whether a team is formed to assist with a specific project such as a product launch or committed to an indefinite, sustainable process in the company, teams expand the horizons of those who serve on them. They help employees step out of their silos and contribute to the larger vision of the company. In a well-composed team, true organizational cross-pollination can take place.

> *Employees that serve on teams develop a broader, bolder perspective.*

Teams are intrinsic to the HOT Plan; the program is built upon them, and the plan itself sets teams up to succeed. In essence, teams are the performance engines of the company.

How We Structure Our Teams

As we mentioned earlier, the HOT Plan is team based. From the long-standing senior leadership team to the most temporary task forces, the HOT Plan structures our company into work groups formed around a set of clearly communicated performance challenges. Our company supports our teams by giving them the resources and time needed to accomplish their goals.

At Pitsco, the HOT Plan harnesses the performance engine of teams from the top to the bottom of the company. The Tribal Council provides executive leadership as a team; interdepartmental HOT Teams carry out cross-company initiatives; departmental HOT Teams fulfill departmental responsibilities under the leadership of their supervisors; and task forces form as temporary teams to perform unique, one-time tasks for the company, such as a system-wide computer update. Because the projects of Pitsco frequently overlap the jurisdiction of several different teams, it is important for teams to communicate and coordinate their work.

Pitsco's Tribal Council

Pitsco's Tribal Council is an indispensable part of the HOT Plan. Because the executive leadership team sets the direction for the company each year and is responsible for the company's most strategic business decisions, the existence of a high-performance leadership team is fundamental. At Pitsco, the Tribal Council is composed of the heads of each of the company's divisions and consists of about 10 members.

Our Tribal Council operates under a simple leadership structure, as do the other HOT Teams. The Tribal Council has a captain, a cocaptain, and a recorder. The team meets weekly to cover progress on the company's Key Initiatives (KIs) and Must Win Challenges (MWCs). In addition to this regular meeting, the team meets daily in a 15-minute stand-up meeting to coordinate information and review various logistical elements of the company.

The number of Must Win Challenges is kept small to make them more achievable.

Once a year Tribal Council works through the process of selecting the MWCs. As mentioned in Chapter 4, these challenges serve as guidelines for company KIs and HOT Targets (HOTs) in the coming year. MWCs are more than grandiose wishes; they are intentions for expansion of the company. An MWC gives particular focus to an area of operations in order to expand its profitability, achieve its full potential, or better fulfill its service to the company's vision.

The number of MWCs is kept small to make them more achievable. Our MWCs number between three and five and frequently carry over from year to year. Recent MWCs at Pitsco include intentions to:

- Increase revenue and profitability.
- Develop products that meet academic standards.
- Enhance customer satisfaction.
- Acquire new customers.
- Share Pitsco success stories internally and externally.

After the MWCs are chosen for the year, usually by early fall at Pitsco, the council breaks them down into KIs, a subject gone over in greater detail in Chapter 6.

Interdepartmental and Departmental HOT Teams and Task Forces

There are two types of HOT Teams: interdepartmental and departmental. Although these teams target company needs in different ways, they are both designed to serve long-term functions within the company. Task forces, on the other hand, are short-term teams that fill the gap for short-term initiatives.

Interdepartmental HOT Teams

Interdepartmental HOT Teams are long-term teams that carry out cross-company initiatives. Though we periodically review HOT Teams to assess whether they have fulfilled their purpose and should be dissolved or replaced with an updated version, most of the needs a HOT Team addresses represent ongoing operations. Therefore, interdepartmental teams tend to have an extended life cycle.

For example, we created sales and finance HOT Teams to assist school districts with funding and/or financing options for major curriculum installations. These types of needs are unlikely to dry up in the near future, so the longevity of these teams is ensured. Longevity of teams is desirable; it produces continuity and equity. The longer team members work together, the more valuable they are as a team because of their accumulated knowledge about their task and each other, as well as their professional relationships and networking outside of the business.

Because of the longevity and influence of an interdepartmental HOT Team, the creation of new HOT Teams is not a casual undertaking. The first question for your company to ask when creating interdepartmental HOT Teams is "How many teams can our company support?"

*Too few teams is as big
a problem as too many.*

Regular workloads must be accomplished even if your employee is on an interdepartmental team. Team members require time away from their daily tasks to carry out the extra responsibilities that HOT Team requires, including team meetings. Supervisors must adjust the workload of team members accordingly.

With HOT Teams, it is just as much a problem to have too many teams as to have too few. If people are spread too thin, teams suffer from under-focused leadership. Lack of team focus undermines the HOT Plan's success. How many teams are ideal? There is no magic formula for the number of teams a business should have, but at Pitsco, which presently employs close to 200 people, we try to keep about 12 active HOT Teams each year.

So let's say you are past that hurdle and know how many teams your company can support. What comes next?

The next step is deciding who should be on the teams. This is not always as simple as it sounds. Gathering the right people for a HOT Team is the key to the team's success and productivity. The people on the team must be able to act independently as they carry out the responsibilities assigned to them, yet function as team players.

It must be acknowledged that although high-performance teams are the engine of business today, not everyone is cut out for teamwork. At Pitsco, we respect these personality differences and attempt to find a job for these individuals where they fit best. Other considerations in successful team building include the size of the team desired and the performance criteria for the job.

Departmental HOT Teams

Departmental HOT Teams are long-term teams that carry out initiatives within specific departments. In the early days, we did not extend the HOTs to departments, but we soon found that teams were needed. Now each of the departments at Pitsco – from Manufacturing to Marketing – also develop HOTs under the guidance of their supervisor. Since we brought the work of departments under the structure of HOTs and HOT Teams, Pitsco supervisors tell us that their workers are more efficient. Departmental HOT Targets also simplify supervisory tasks by giving clear direction and benchmarks for each person's work.

Temporary Task Forces

Short-term tasks that require a team solution do not fit the long-term HOT Team model. Tasks like these are carried out by task forces.

Lisa, our president, saw the perfect opportunity to create a task force to fully address an update in Payment Card Industry (PCI) compliance. New PCI rules and regulations would affect on-campus security. Lisa created a task force that was very broad and cross-functional. Once the new regulations were implemented across all departments, the task force dissolved.

> *Replace teams with task forces when working on a temporary job.*

It is important to note that *task forces formed for temporary work objectives do not earn HOT Points* even though they complete tasks in a team format. Once the task force work is completed, the task force is discontinued. The HOT Point system is not designed for short-term applications.

How to Choose the Right Team

How do you know who the right people for your interdepartmental HOT Teams are? We've found the following guidelines for team member selection to be effective:

1. Skills are important, but don't overemphasize them in team member selection.

Of greater importance than raw skill is the concern that the right cross-section of departments is represented. While skills are a consideration, other aspects – complementary perspectives, personality types, eagerness to participate, and creative thinking – are equally important. In fact, these latter qualities are more difficult to find than trainable skills and therefore are often more valuable.

2. Limit individual involvement to two or three teams.

Every team assignment adds responsibilities to your employees' workload. I learned while coaching the Weleetka track team that you can lose good people by asking too much of them. Also, there is a law of diminishing returns: the more teams a person is on, the less focus they have to offer each group. But there is a balance to this: overlapping team members help the cross-pollination of ideas across the company. Also, some people are bridge builders by nature; serving on more than one team enables these valuable players to put their strengths to work by building bridges between groups and strengthening the connections in the company.

> *Serving on more than one team allows natural bridge builders to put their strengths to work in your company culture.*

3. Limit team size to no more than 10 people.

This rule might have to be fudged from time to time, but the advantages of smaller teams are many. Smaller teams are more flexible, efficient, and focused. Larger teams are harder to handle logistically, and sometimes the division of responsibilities becomes less clear in a larger team. The individual's voice is harder to hear in larger groups; the extroverts tend to get more floor time while the introverts step aside. I think teams of seven or eight are the most dynamic.

4. Aim for a strong mix of both men and women on teams.

Various studies have indicated that different genders approach problem solving from very different viewpoints. This diversity is valuable on HOT Teams. A strong gender mix is a frequently overlooked aspect of team building and should be consciously addressed. The varying perspectives in this mix inevitably lead to far better dialogue and superior solutions.

Guidelines for Choosing HOT Team Leaders

1. It is most important that team leaders be good listeners and have previous leadership experience in the company.

Team leaders must facilitate well, but they also need to see the bigger picture and have a proven ability to think outside of their own niche. Good familiarity with an overall view of products, processes, and the vision of the company is obviously important, but keep in mind that team members acquire a bigger picture simply as a result of being on a HOT Team. Heading a HOT Team provides an opportunity to develop key employees and also train them for further leadership.

2. A team leader should be someone who can receive and learn from the ideas of others.

Leaders must embrace the vision of developing others, not just focusing on their own advancement. To do this, leaders must practice stepping back and allowing others to take the lead. Teams are all about using collaboration to achieve HOTs.

3. Place a Tribal Council member on each team, but do not make him or her the leader of the team.

We haven't always placed a Tribal Council member on each team, but it is a good idea when possible. A Tribal Council member on each team has the potential to bring a broader perspective to the team and help keep the vision in focus. He or she also can bring the team's insights back to Tribal Council. Of course, all HOT Teams send minutes of their meetings to Tribal, but written minutes can't capture the nuances of discussion and team dynamics.

Team Organization and Accountability

Consistency of proven processes in any business is a key element of success, and the operation of HOT Teams is no exception.

HOT Team meetings need to be scheduled regularly, at a specific location and time, once or twice a month. Semimonthly meetings last an hour; less-frequent meetings may be up to 90 minutes long, and, as mentioned earlier, stand-up meetings last 15 minutes. These meetings are an important daily addition for our Tribal Council and other very active HOT Teams.

The regularity of meetings is an important factor in the success of HOT Teams.

The regularity of meetings is an important factor in the success of HOT Teams. The proactive work of the team requires consistent meeting times, and the members' schedules must provide for that. Being proactive means staying on top of work, and regular meetings keep everyone on task. Regular meetings also make it easier for people to create their schedules around the work of the team, an important factor in high team cohesion.

The team stays accountable to Tribal Council not only through its HOTs but also by the team recorder submitting minutes of the meetings to Tribal Council. We have found it useful to use a standardized format for minutes. All of our teams use the same minutes template for recording what happens in their meetings. Not only does the template capture meeting data in a streamlined way, it also guides the discussion itself by emphasizing the weight of certain activities.

The HOT Team Minutes template (Appendix II) includes:

- Action Items Update (old business and workflow)
- New Business (discussion notes)
- Action Items (upcoming deadlines sorted by due date and identified by who is responsible)

The recorder for each team submits minutes to Tribal Council and team members within 48 hours of the meeting.

Disbanding Teams

About once a year, Tribal Council evaluates the teams to see what is working, what is not, which teams should continue, and which should be dissolved. This scrutiny is a normal – and necessary – part of the life cycle of a team. The council reviews all the current HOT Teams, their efficiency, results, and impact.

It is a disservice to your company to drag a team out through a long, slow demise.

If teams are no longer working efficiently, they are evaluated on several levels. Is it a personnel issue? Overburdened leadership? Did the personalities on the team fail to produce the right dynamics? Sometimes the problem is deeper than that.

A good example of a deeper problem occurred when Pitsco once formed a team called Corporate Services. At the time it seemed like a fine idea – bringing together Accounting, IT, and Human Resources. We all had high hopes for this team. But after a number of meetings, we had to admit that the team wasn't doing anything unique. The question "What are we supposed to be doing?" hung over this team's meetings like a cloud. Team members themselves chose to disband and Tribal Council finalized it. Admitting that a team concept is unsound is a little painful, but once the fact that a team has outlived its usefulness is recognized, it is a disservice to your company and to everyone on the team to drag a team out through a long, slow demise.

Sustaining High-Performance Teams

If high-performance teams are the engine of success for your business, what does it take to keep that engine running at peak performance? Rewards, recognition, and collaborative support, say authors Glenn Parker, Jerry McAdams, and David Zielinski in their book *Rewarding Teams: Lessons from the Trenches*.[22]

In *Rewarding Teams*, the authors examine 27 detailed case studies of companies that have designed and implemented effective team systems. Similar to Katzenbach and Smith, their conclusion is that effective business teams are not add-ons to the main program; instead, they are embedded in the organizational culture of the business. The symbols, rituals, rewards, stories, myths, and heroes of the business should all support teamwork. Rewards and recognition should also be aligned to promote the work of your teams.

Integrate everything in the organizational structure to support the function of teams.

According to Parker, McAdams, and Zielinski, all teams eventually come up against a variety of environmental obstacles. The key to moving forward is to remove as many obstacles as possible by integrating everything in the organizational structure to support the function of teams.

This integration has many faces. Sometimes it may be in how things get done, while other times it may be through celebrations and community service. One way the HOT Plan aligns the culture of collaboration is through frequent celebration of team achievements. Monthly company-wide meetings for all staff, led by the executive leadership team, not only report company numbers but also recognize teams that have done outstanding work with certificates of achievement and gift cards. Collegiality also can be integrated through monthly luncheon celebrations of employee birthdays. We provide community service opportunities for individuals and teams that they can count as HOT Points.

Ultimately, teams work. But engines need a vehicle, and in the HOT Plan, it is the HOTs that provide the vehicle to drive success home.

Chapter Eight

HOT Targets

I t happened again just the other day.

"So, what do you do at Pitsco?" a new acquaintance asked at a business networking event.

He was just making small talk and being polite, but there I was again, face to face with my eternal conversational conundrum, wondering exactly what to say.

Where do I begin to make small talk about our increasingly complex work? There isn't a good one- or two-sentence synopsis that captures the diversity of our operations today. As a business owner, I am not alone in struggling with this; any owner of a lively, profitable company soon finds himself or herself in the same predicament. A growing business soon defies small talk summaries as it steps into the whirlwind of production, cash flow, people challenges, sales pipelines, pending contracts, new ideas, marketing, distribution, and much more.

"Our vision is leading education that positively affects learners," I finally replied. "We are STEM education leaders and sell our products all over the world. But helping teachers and students is where our heart is and will always be."

An important key to success is not to get blown off course by the whirlwind of business activity. As your business grows, you must ensure that all the moving parts of your organization stay in sync, moving together toward the accomplishment of a unified vision.

The HOT Plan manages this process through the use of goals called HOT Targets (HOTs). As we discussed in Chapter 6, HOT Teams write them as bite-size goals and assign them deadlines. It is the HOTs that translate Must Win Challenges (MWCs) and Key Initiatives (KIs) into doable steps.

But how do you write effective, efficient HOTs? These goals have the power to define your company's activity and synchronize the efforts of your teams as they work together to accomplish the MWCs for the year. Let's look at the process step by step. For our discussion, the terms *goals*, *targets*, and *HOTs* are used interchangeably.

The Annual Timeline

HOTs, or goals written with the precision of targets, are woven into the very ethos of Pitsco. Creating highly effective HOTs has been an evolving process for us. When we began the HOT Plan, we used standard goal-writing guidelines. Today, our process for writing HOTs is much more efficient, refined through nearly 20 years of continuous improvement. The first step begins with the annual timeline.

Each year when we write HOTs, we follow a timeline that is designed to ensure our employees are not rushed in the goal-setting process. Tribal Council begins evaluating the coming year's MWCs in late summer. Then, Tribal develops a dozen or more KIs to coordinate with them. Tribal completes this process by early fall (see Chapter 6).

We then communicate MWCs and KIs to HOT Team leaders and department supervisors, who in turn lead their teams and departments in writing HOTs for the coming year. All team members assist in writing the HOTs, which they complete and turn in by December.

HOT Targets are woven into the very ethos of the company.

Each Tribal Council member supervises certain HOT Teams. As each team turns in HOTs and Tribal approves them and adds them to the company-wide list, a sort of road map emerges for the year ahead. By the time employees leave for Christmas break, all the HOTs are posted on the company intranet, enabling employees to see exactly where their work will focus when they return in January. This process helps each person begin the new year with a strong sense of ownership of the company's direction and a clear view of what to expect. MWCs, KIs, and HOTs work together to pave a focused, profitable, and meaningful pathway for the coming year.

Preparing Supervisors for Success

Pitsco invests a significant amount of time in making sure the MWCs and KIs are well communicated to the supervisors, who will lead the planning of HOTs with their teams. Tribal Council holds special supervisor training meetings to outline the MWCs and KIs. Tribal uses a conversational approach to communicate these focus points and holds a group discussion about the meaning and purpose of each MWC and KI. We ask team leaders and supervisors to follow this same process when they present the MWCs and KIs to their HOT Teams and departments.

HOT Target Guidelines

As we discussed in Chapter 6, HOTs translate MWCs and KIs into bite-size, action-oriented, and time-framed tasks. We prefer the word *targets* instead of *goals* because it communicates both precision and action. The term *goal* can mean many things to many people, sometimes representing ultimate ideals rather than plans of action. HOTs, on the other hand, are goals we write with the precision of a target. On the archery range, targets have a bull's-eye and when you aim at a target, the bull's-eye is in the crosshairs. The evidence of your shot is immediately obvious; you either hit the bull's-eye or you don't.

Each HOT is written with a bull's-eye. Each HOT states **who** is responsible to hit the target, **what** exactly is to be accomplished, **when** it will be completed, and **how** to know that the target has been hit, based on evidence of accomplishment. These four questions – **the WWWH of HOTs** – add precision and clarity to HOT Targets.

The HOT Plan's four essential questions – **Who, What, When,** and **How?** – might look something like this in practice:

The HOT Plan's Four Essential Questions

Who?	Give the name of the HOT Team or subgroup within the team: "The video editors …"
What?	Define what is to be accomplished: "… will complete 10-minute videos for the annual meeting …"
When?	Give a specific completion date: "… by December 15 …"
How?	Provide the evidence (benchmark) of success: "… as evidenced by a showing at the annual meeting on December 20."

The process of creating goals that touch on each of these points was greatly simplified by the addition of database software we developed, *HOTware*™. *HOTware* is made available to each team and provides prompts to assist in writing HOTs according to guidelines. In addition, *HOTware* provides additional guidelines, such as identifying how each HOT lines up with the MWCs and KIs, the number of points that should be assigned for each HOT, and the names of who supervises the target's completion.

All of the work in your company, from day-to-day routines to innovative projects, is eligible to be written as a HOT, but not everything is suitable. HOTs must be both meaningful and doable. Two guidelines we suggest are that the task should not be so small as to indicate trivial accomplishments, nor so big that it cannot be completed within a reasonable time frame.

HOT Points

HOT Points are the basis for the annual HOT Check and keep the entire system moving forward. In the beginning, we were not sure how to go about this in a fair way. Our HOT Champion and CEO collaborated on point values after the targets were submitted to ensure fairness – taking into account time involved and the complexity of the task. Over time, however, patterns emerged that made assigning points a more uniform process.

Based on these patterns, we created a simple, time-based point scale that could be made available on our company intranet and could be used by supervisors and their teams in the planning stage of points.

Now, when supervisors submit targets for approval, the projected number of points is already attached so that targets and points are negotiated for approval at the same time.

The following chart is now used to determine HOT Points:

Time to Complete	Points
8 hours or less	2
9-16 hours	3
17-40 hours	4
41-80 hours	5
81-120 hours	6
121-160 hours	8
1-3 months	10
3-6 months	12
All year	15

Four Types of HOTs

As mentioned in Chapter 6, there are four types of HOTs: Operational HOTs, Above-and-Beyond HOTs, Cultural HOTs, and Open HOTs.

Operational HOTs

Operational HOTs: projects and work milestones that are completed in the course of a normal year.

- *A majority of HOTs declared by teams will be Operational HOTs.*

- *Operational HOTs are often similar from year to year.*

For most departments and teams, the greatest share of HOTs will be Operational HOTs. Operational HOTs pertain to the normal operations and production within the company. These goals target regular work done to maintain a business. Most recurring events in normal operations and upkeep can be written as Operational HOTs, and there will be very few changes from year to year. Because of this, *HOTware* provides a drop-down menu in the goal-planning section of the database in order to simplify goal-setting.

At Pitsco, an example of an Operational HOT is the process of publishing our external-audience magazine, *The Pitsco Network*. Our Communications Department publishes and distributes the magazine five times a year. For each issue, the department submits one Operational HOT that overviews the publication process. These five HOTs are worded identically; only the due date changes.

For example, the Operational HOT for a February-March issue of *The Pitsco Network* reads something like this:

"**(1) Who** The Communications Team **(2) What** will produce and distribute the February-March issue of *The Pitsco Network* magazine **(3) When** by February 15, **(4) How** as evidenced by the distribution of the February-March issue."

The Pitsco Network is always due on the 15th of the first month in the two-month cycle. This is an example of an Operational HOT that easily is carried forward. It also illustrates a HOT that focuses on the big picture and leaves the minutiae of the process to the internal daily workings of the staff; this helps the HOT avoid becoming mired in trivial details.

Sample Operational HOTs

Marketing	**(1) Who** The editorial director **(2) What** will update the TETRIX PRIME brochure **(3) When** by July 15, **(4) How** as evidenced by providing an updated brochure PDF to the vice president of sales for review.
Machine Shop	**(1) Who** The machine shop supervisor **(2) What** will compile an itemized list of equipment needs **(3) When** by September 30, **(4) How** as evidenced by submitting the list to the company president.
Media Relations	**(1) Who** The marketing director **(2) What** will develop an updated convention calendar for the upcoming year **(3) When** by November 30, **(4) How** as evidenced by presenting the calendar to the vice president of sales.

Above-and-Beyond HOTs

Above-and-Beyond HOTs: commitments that exceed what a particular job requires.

- *Above-and-Beyond HOTs can involve pioneering new processes, exploring new areas of development, or reaching new heights in a current process.*

- *We encourage teams at all levels of the organization to be creative as they develop Above-and-Beyond HOTs.*

While Operational HOTs address the basic work requirements in an organization, Above-and-Beyond HOTs address aspirations. These HOTs arise from a team's determination to exceed requirements, to stretch themselves, and to enter a new sphere within their area of expertise. When teams create Above-and-Beyond HOTs, they commit to contribute in an exceptional way.

Above-and-Beyond HOT guidelines prompt questions like these:

- What new service could we provide to customers or to other departments?
- What new process can we implement that will multiply our team's efficiency?
- How can we increase our company's visibility and boost customer satisfaction?

Asking teams to think of ways they can go above-and-beyond the normal routine of their work might sound vague, but this type of request opens the doors of imagination and engages the highest levels of creative thinking. Once employees know we welcome their most ambitious ideas and take them seriously, fresh thinking abounds.

Sadly, many companies never benefit from this overflow because they never invite employees to engage in above-and-beyond thinking; in fact, in some companies shun employee ideas. This is a sad fact when you consider that employees are usually an organization's best resource for above-and-beyond thinking.

I strongly suggest that supervisors and team leaders mine this valuable resource by using Above-and-Beyond HOTs to solicit employee suggestions. Although there always will be some employees who grumble, most will feel honored that their employer values their creativity and requests their ideas. Encouraging employees to share insights fosters an independence of mind that leads to proactive behavior. Leadership is born from such thinking.

How many Above-and-Beyond HOTs should there be? There is no particular number or percentage, but be prepared to pare down a long list. Ideas seem to percolate and soon overflow, often multiplying to the point that they cannot possibly all be accomplished within one time frame. Chances are that your team will have to choose which ideas it can realistically accomplish.

Sample Above-and-Beyond HOTs

Editing Team	**(1) Who** Editors **(2) What** will review the criteria for product testing in the handbook of the Quality Assurance Department **(3) When** by January 30, **(4) How** as evidenced by sending a summary of their recommendations to the editing coordinator.
Plastics Team	**(1) Who** The Plastics Team **(2) What** will realign the match between the bi-wheel mold halves **(3) When** by March 30, **(4) How** as evidenced by the achievement of the clamping tolerance to the bi-wheel mold.
Sales Team	**(1) Who** The Sales Team **(2) What** will create an action plan for reengaging 25 inactive customers **(3) When** by January 20, **(4) How** as evidenced by submitting the plan to sales and marketing managers.

Cultural HOTs

Cultural HOTs: targets that enhance the quality of life in the internal community of your business and in the external communities to which your business belongs.

- *Cultural HOTs can be directed internally or externally; they can be local or global.*

- *Cultural HOTs provide bonding opportunities among staff members through accomplishing service work together, supporting each other in practical ways, and sharing meaningful celebrations of what has been accomplished.*

I deeply believe that every company must consider how it can make the world a better place, but this often is hard to quantify. One of the best ways to translate the lofty value of making the world a better place into an accomplishment is through the use of Cultural HOTs.

Cultural HOTs aren't about widgets and dollars; they are about meaning and purpose.

To be honest, making the world a better place was not on my list of goals for Pitsco at the outset; even influencing the local community positively wasn't in my orbit. My biggest initial concern was making sure my company survived. In fact, most entrepreneurs and business owners will tell you that survival was their initial focus as well, if they are completely honest. But eventually the startup phase is complete and it is good to broaden your business focus with Cultural HOTs. If you don't know where to begin, just ask your employees. They will lead the way.

"All these positive vibes are great," you may be thinking, "but how does this increase your bottom-line profits?"

I could mount a solid argument that Cultural HOTs do, in fact, increase the bottom line by fostering employee engagement, team building, community loyalty, and other factors that lead to expanded sales.

But I won't. That really isn't what Cultural HOTs are all about.

Cultural HOTs aren't about widgets and dollars. They are about meaning and purpose. Cultural HOTs foster a vital social bond between employees and also create an emotional connection between employees and their work, a connection identified as essential to employee satisfaction and retention, especially among millennial workers.[23]

Employees quickly grasp the concept of Cultural HOTs and will often surprise you with their creativity and enthusiasm for these types of goals. Today, Cultural HOTs are firmly ensconced in Pitsco's HOT Plan. Each year, all of our HOT Teams come up with a minimum of two cultural goals: one relating to the internal community of our company and one relating to the external community.

Sample Cultural HOTs

Internal Cultural Goals

Logistics Team	**(1) Who** The Logistics Team **(2) What** will participate in a company landscape cleanup **(3) When** by March 15, **(4) How** as evidenced by a report about the project in the April team meeting.
Media Relations Team	**(1) Who** The Media Relations Team **(2) What** will organize company-wide family pictures **(3) When** by March 31, **(4) How** as evidenced by picture distribution on May 31.

External Cultural Goals

Shipping and Receiving Team	**(1) Who** The Shipping and Receiving Team **(2) What** will coordinate a toy drive for a children's hospital **(3) When** during the month of November, **(4) How** as evidenced by a report on the toy drive in December's team meeting minutes and a picture of the distribution at the hospital.

Internal Cultural HOTs can cover everything from staff baby showers to hosting a Christmas party for staff children or grandchildren. External Cultural HOTs can include such things as charitable projects, scholarship fund-raisers, or even building a float for our community's Christmas parade. When complete, such accomplishments often result in a party to celebrate – something natural and fun for everyone involved. But even more significant is the sense of family that this fosters among employees over time.

Fulfilling Cultural HOTs also broadens the scope of vision among your employees that the work they do has a purpose beyond the company. This is a powerful asset.

Open HOTs

Open HOTs: HOTs that make room for the unexpected. This category of HOTs exists to capture the opportunities that arise during the current year that were not possible to anticipate during the planning months of the year prior.

- *Every department in your organization will encounter situations that can prompt Open HOTs.*
- *Open HOTs make a way for employees to get credit for investing themselves in unanticipated opportunities.*

If you are familiar with the year-to-year operations of any complex organization, you may be thinking that there is a glaring omission in the HOT Plan. Creating a master plan at the beginning of the year that accounts for all the big projects of the upcoming year is a fine thing. But new opportunities appear out of left field each and every year, and wrenches are thrown into even the best of plans. When the unexpected happens, plans must be revised on the fly. How does the HOT Plan remain flexible enough to accommodate this? Open HOTs fill the gap between the master plan and the unexpected.

Open HOTs balance the need to plan ahead with the need to be flexible. They cover not only the unexpected but also projects that could not be formally declared by the annual HOTs deadline because all of the factors were not yet in place. Open HOTs allow for the opportunity to add those projects back into the schedule when the time is right.

Because every active department and team will have such opportunities, I ask every department at our company to submit 12 open points each year to be applied to unanticipated work. You may choose a different number of Open HOT Points, but however many points you choose, just do it. Good employees who take care of unplanned challenges and opportunities will only get credit for their contribution if you have a system of Open HOTs.

Sample Open HOTs

Graphics Team	**(1) Who** The graphic artists **(2) What** will create the graphics for materials at the East Coast Farmers' Expo **(3) When** by May 31, **(4) How** as evidenced by artwork submitted to the Marketing Team.
Accounting Team	**(1) Who** The accounting staff **(2) What** will prepare a report explaining the impact of the new taxation guidelines on our company **(3) When** by June 15, **(4) How** as evidenced by presenting the report at the July planning meeting.
Maintenance Team	**(1) Who** The maintenance staff **(2) What** will clean gravel off the parking lot **(3) When** two days after the completion of the asphalt recoat, **(4) How** as evidenced by submitting a completed work order to Tribal Council.

Even when you have established Open HOTs, most of the unexpected work goes underreported. That means loyal employees cover the bases to keep things running smoothly, but points they are eligible to capture for that work will not be included in the end-of-year bonus calculation. Thereby, their extra work will go unrewarded.

This is why we urge members of our organization – frequently! – to claim Open HOTs for unexpected work. If at the end of a year you discover that you have a deficit of Open HOTs, get the word out about the missed points – and the missed bonus money. Perhaps this will help inspire a few cheerleaders in your company to keep everyone on task next year in submitting Open HOTs.

Creating HOT Fun

When all is said and done, writing HOTs is a fun process. Personnel from all levels of the company have an opportunity to give input and participate in mapping out the company agenda for the coming year. The process is engaging; it involves a great deal of creative energy and provides an ideal opportunity for all ideas to be heard. Submitting an idea as a possible HOT doesn't guarantee that it will be approved, but it does guarantee that it will be seriously considered. Keeping good faith with employees by considering each and every idea submitted is essential to employee buy-in and optimum performance.

> *The creation of HOTs is the perfect time for everyone's ideas to be heard.*

As we mentioned earlier, HOT Teams are the engine of performance in our company, and HOTs provide a reliable vehicle to drive success home. But who has the keys to the car?

Chapter Nine

HOT Accountability

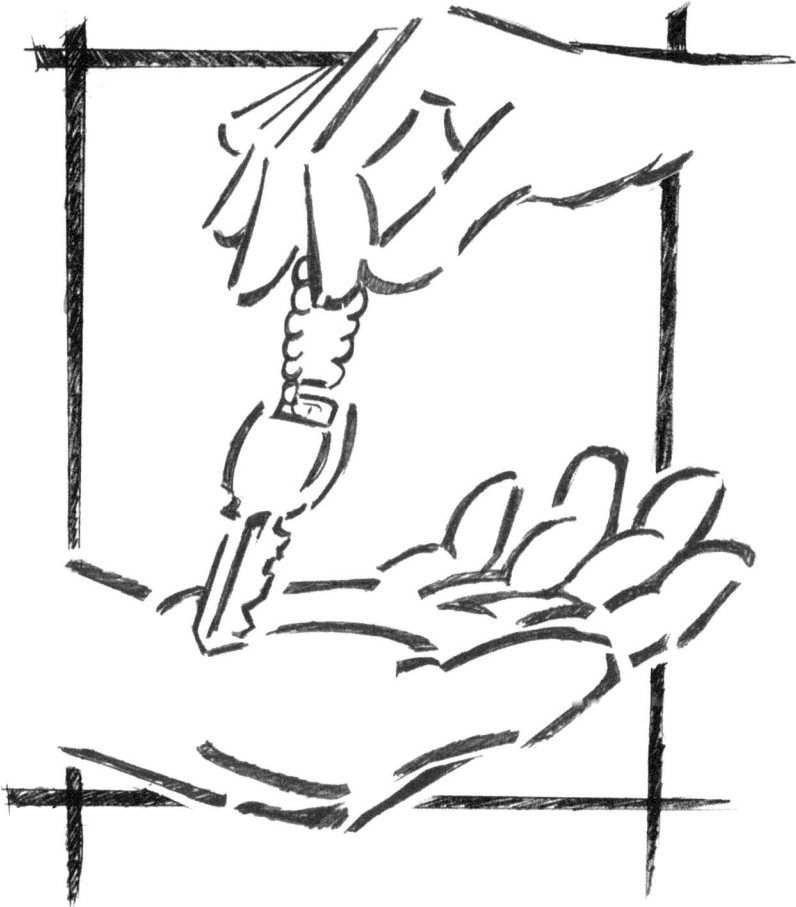

I like to see the good in people.

It is my belief that most people truly want to do a good job. Maybe some people are motivated to do a good job because they see their work as a reflection of themselves. Perhaps others simply find joy in the aesthetic sense of a job well done. Either way, when involved with work or projects they care about, most people love to excel.

But even when motivated, nearly everyone needs some form of accountability to do their best work in a timely manner. Accountability is more than answering to someone else or meeting a deadline; accountability is about positive touch points such as coaching for excellence, supervision, guidance, and timelines that give both context and closure to projects.

There is great positive power in accountability.

Accountability, in its purest sense, is a natural by-product of a relationship. The moment we accept responsibility for a task and the workflow begins, accountability is in the grain. When we agree to produce a product or provide a service for someone else, and they agree to compensate us for our efforts, there is an expectation on both sides. This is positive accountability, and accountability is the key to the car that drives success home.

Positive accountability systems translate expectation into a partnership of accomplishment. The best positive accountability systems draw out the passionate, creative energy in your workforce.

Unfortunately, accountability systems are not always positive, however, and the worst systems involve coercion backed by threats. These images of accountability are so pervasive that when a random sample of workers were asked to define the word *accountability* in an informal survey conducted by the authors of *The Oz Principle: Getting*

Results Through Individual and Organizational Accountability, most of the employees interviewed replied with negative definitions. Respondents defined accountability as, among other things, "something that happens to you when things go wrong," "paying the piper," or "a tool that management uses to pressure people to perform."[24]

Certainly, at the most basic level, the purpose of any accountability system is to make sure work gets done on time, in an orderly manner, and with satisfactory quality. But good accountability systems go beyond monitoring and nudging; good systems empower greatness. When structured properly, an accountability system helps people take charge of their outcomes and can even inspire them to raise the bar on their work's quality. The best systems cast accountability in the context of vision. Visionary management recognizes that accountability itself has the ability to unlock the intelligence and talent of employees by granting them *the gift of responsibility*.

Gifting responsibility to your employees is more than a new name for accountability. Gifting responsibility extends the locus of responsibility to employees so they can take charge of their work. It also involves providing them with the matrix of support necessary to do their job well. The matrix of support includes any additional training needed, reasonable scheduling and workload, adequate timelines and staffing to accomplish the work, and all the tools necessary to do the job well.

Gifting responsibility goes beyond quotas and deadlines.

Accountability that moves the locus of responsibility to employees begins the process with Who and How questions. These simple questions provide a foundational clarity to the work:

- Who is responsible for what?
- How are they to carry out their responsibilities?
- How will the progress flow across the organization be tracked?

In very small businesses or organizations, a committed solitary worker toiling away at a one-person project may carry the answers to all of these questions, seeing the project through from start to finish. But in larger organizations, projects usually involve multiple players. And in today's global marketplace, these players may be scattered across the world. This makes accountability an essential part of the process. A multi-person project requires a plan to manage workflow through deadlines, timelines, well-defined roles, and clear evidence of a goal's completion so that all team members – regardless of their location – can keep the job on track and bring it to completion.

Employees gain a greater sense of ownership of their work when given the locus of responsibility.

Accountability in multiplayer projects is the process by which all players communicate – by which all know what is expected of them and the benchmarks that indicate they have met those expectations. The gift of responsibility empowers employees by giving clarity to the assignment, the opportunity to take responsibility for the work, and the resources necessary to accomplish it on time.

As mentioned in Chapter 3, employees gain a greater sense of ownership of their work when given the locus of responsibility. Responsibility and ownership walk hand in hand – a fact long recognized by the finance and home mortgage industry. It is commonly known that home ownership increases citizen responsibility, improves social outcomes, and undergirds the very success of communities.[25]

In a similar way, ownership of the company's success is known to increase employee responsibility.

The accountability process of the HOT Plan, gifting responsibility, is the underlying mechanism by which the whole system operates. It provides ownership and in so doing increases employee responsibility, improves relationships across all levels of the company, and undergirds the success of your organization's culture.

Building the Matrix of Support

A matrix of support for your employees begins with clear, well-communicated processes of how things get done in your organization.

When an accountability system is built upon well-defined processes, not the power or rank of someone in management, it is easy to understand and follow. As discussed in Chapter 2, clarified lines of responsibility build confidence in the workplace. Well-defined processes ensure that the freedom and autonomy of employees are protected.

In summary, here are eight important questions about accountability and the processes of the HOT Plan.

1. How do HOT Targets (HOTs) provide teams with a process of accountability for the company's Key Initiatives (KIs)?

In Chapter 8 we detail how each team or department devises its HOTs. Tribal Council informs the supervisors and team leaders of the Must Win Challenges (MWCs) and KIs for the year, but the team itself writes HOTs using the WWWH model. Later, a goal-review process with the HOT Champion provides a cross-check and any necessary revisions of HOTs.

2. How do these HOTs provide a process of accountability between different teams?

In Chapters 7 and 12, we discuss how HOTs connect and flow across groups, directed by supervisors and team leaders under the oversight of the HOT Champion. Each team must make sure their projects are coordinated with other departments and that timelines sync up. Later, the HOT Champion reviews the company-wide big picture and the timeline to double-check the workflow of HOTs.

3. How do HOTs provide accountability in the completion of work?

Chapter 8 defines the WWWH of HOTs and carefully spells out the evidence for target completion.

4. How does the accountability of the HOT Plan promote employee growth and creativity?

The HOT Plan provides two types of HOTs that build in a process for promoting employee growth and creativity. First, Above-and-Beyond HOTs promote employee growth and creativity by encouraging employees to expand their day-to-day roles and explore new ideas, implement experimental changes, take on projects they've been craving to sink their teeth into, or even become trained in new skills. Second, Cultural HOTs promote personal growth and creativity through community outreach and service.

5. What is the accountability process for tracking team progress?

Team leaders are responsible for reporting their progress throughout the year by logging into the *HOTware*™ database and reporting their target as completed. They report when HOTs are completed or if they have run into a problem and need to renegotiate the completion date of a goal.

6. What process tracks the organization's progress as a whole?

At Pitsco, we print a chart monthly that summarizes the progress being made company-wide toward the completion of HOTs. We also make the full data of every team's individual progress available in the *HOTware* database, which all employees can access. This has the benefit of providing complete organizational transparency.

7. What is the process when HOTs need to be modified?

Teams can appeal to the HOT Champion to have HOT deadlines altered during the course of the year if circumstances render the original deadline unreachable. The teams must present a good case for the requested change, but flexibility is maintained.

8. How does our accountability system ensure that people are recognized for their accomplishments?

The HOT Plan calls for clarification, transparency, and celebration of accomplishments, a process that provides opportunities for supervisors to give day-to-day employee recognition. Annually, the process for recognition of employee accomplishments is the HOT Check. As touched on in Chapters 5, 7, 8, and 13, targets are worth points, and every employee gets the same-size bonus check, based on the accumulation of points through successfully completed targets. The HOT Check gives a tangible way to share the satisfaction of a job well done. Employees tell us the HOT Check helps them keep HOTs on the radar throughout the year.

The Gift That Challenges

The idea of gifting responsibility to employees is challenging to some employers. Why? Because although gifting responsibility increases accountability, it also increases employee influence in the processes of how things get done. This is a culture shift for many businesses; inviting employees to have more input and influence in how things get done makes many employers a little nervous. Yes, your employees will undoubtedly see things differently than management does. Implementing changes based on employee ideas can feel like giving away management's power. Yet the opposite is true. When change based on employee input is implemented, power increases for management. Why is this? Because respect is increased, and the respect of employees grants credibility to management.

Basic logic tells us that in any field of endeavor, it is the ones doing the work, the ones who are hands on with the process, that understand it best. This is a fundamental truth. But this truth has a corollary: the ones who are in administration – the team coaches and managers – see the big picture best. They are hands on with the overview of the team's work and how it is fitting in with the ultimate goal of the organization.

> *Extending influence to your employees empowers the entire organization.*

Because of these complementary perspectives, an open and ongoing conversation between different levels of your organization is necessary. Such a conversation enables the company to take full advantage of the collective genius of your group. The accountability processes of the HOT Plan open up that conversation.

Opening a conversation is an unusual benefit for an accountability system. As I have observed accountability systems over the years, most are heavy-handed and tend to shut down conversations rather than open them up between management and employees. Perhaps this is because most accountability systems are based on the one-way communication that begins with management asking a question rooted in mistrust: "Did you meet the quota by deadline?" The answer is yes or no, and obviously, no matter how many words are exchanged as to whether or not the quota was met on time, this is not a true conversation.

A true conversation occurs only when ideas are shared back and forth. A conversation begins with mutual respect and trust.

Listen for the Voice

Trust the wisdom of those at all levels of your organization. Who knows better than individual workers how to get their job done? Every craftsperson is conversant with the essential truths of their craft because they experience the substance of their labor with their own minds and hands; they feel it shape at their touch and push back against their will. The expertise of the individual worker is best illustrated in the work of sculptors. Sculptors understand their medium with both their head and heart. When they consider a new project, they take into consideration both the limitations and potential of their medium. It has often been said that the sculptor's stone has a voice of its own, a voice that speaks to the artist about the shapes hidden in the stone and how to set them free. True artists listen for the voice of their work. To help artists excel, we do not tell them how to sculpt. Instead, we support them in their work and provide a framework within which they can accomplish it. This is a good metaphor for all types of work.

Trust the wisdom of those at all levels of your organization.

Understanding the voice of their work is necessary for those in all fields of labor, not just the arts, according to Matthew Crawford in his book *Shop Class as Soulcraft: An Inquiry into the Value of Work*.[26] Whether people are car mechanics, accountants, welders, or electricians, Crawford sees special virtues in working with material objects: electrical wires, hand tools, wood, and steel. To Crawford, the unambiguous realities of material things make accountability immediately apparent – something he admires. Here, he addresses the experiences of the mechanic:

"The intellectual virtue of judging things rightly [for the mechanic] … is typically not the product of detached contemplation. It seems to require that the user of a machine have something at stake, an *interest* of the sort that arises through bodily immersion in some hard reality, the kind that kicks back."[27]

Crawford clearly is skeptical of accountability that arises from the "detached contemplation" of "knowledge work" – labor created from the intellect, from thought alone. His time as a director at a Washington, D.C. think tank and as a writer in a cubicle for an information-services company left him disenchanted with knowledge work. He tells stories of lunching with coworkers who felt their human limitations and intellect were disrespected and therefore had little sense of accountability for the integrity of their work – its intellectual quality or its deadlines. These workers intentionally sabotaged their employers in subtle – and very intelligent – ways.

"One [of the saboteurs] was from my group, a laconic, disheveled man named Mike, whom I liked instantly. He did about as well on his quota as I did on mine (which was not very well), but it didn't seem to bother him too much. Over lunch Mike would recount the outrageous things he had written in his abstracts, which were then published under the names of untenured assistant professors. I could see my own future in such furtive moments of sabotage – the compensating pleasures of a cubicle drone."[28]

The gift of responsibility requires a matrix of support.

The organizations that employed Crawford and his coworkers made the error of not properly valuing the talent and knowledge their employees possessed about their craft – research and writing. The essential conversations did not take place in that organization. The support needed by the writers in order to produce cutting-edge abstracts, reliable research, and impeccable scholarship should have been the subject of a fruitful discussion between management and the writers. Instead of conversation, there were decrees of expectations for a quantity of work that could not be met by such aggressive deadlines. Writers were ordered to produce large amounts of research and writing on short deadlines that made quality work impossible. The think tank writers were not naïve; they were *expert writers and researchers*. As experts, they understood the disparity between the scholarly image of the think tank's work and the less-than-excellent quality of the work they could produce under these limitations. Consequently, their work seemed undervalued, unreal, and even absurd. And that is exactly how they began to treat it.

Maximize Your Greatest Resource

It is impossible for employees to be truly accountable for work under circumstances that do not support them. Crawford condemns the tendency of many organizations to promote innovation and creativity to their staff but give employees no real opportunity to achieve either. Often, leadership in such companies talks up the ideals of production quotas and accountability with guilt-producing rhetoric that places all the responsibility for performance on the employee. The rhetoric rings hollow when it is not followed through by listening carefully to employees to find out what type of support they need to do their best work. The gift of responsibility is not truly granted unless the matrix of support is supplied.

> *Good employees are your*
> *greatest resource.*

If you want the best from your employees and if you want employees to be highly accountable for their work, you must supply the resources they need to get the job done. Think about resources broadly; resources include time, adequate staff support to accomplish what you are asking of them, continual professional development, and the best tools you can afford – whether that is software, computers, or a piece of heavy equipment in manufacturing.

Good employees are your greatest resource. Positive accountability is based on recognition and respect of that fact and begins in the context of relationship between the people on all levels of your company. This type of accountability unlocks the genius and talent of your employees and sets up an efficient workflow in your company. Accountability, like steel infrastructure in a building, provides support for your entire organization. Strengthen your productivity and keep your talent with positive accountability.

Part III. HOT Leaders

Chapters

Chapter Ten

HOT Champion

For any cause to succeed, it must have a champion.

What do we mean by a champion? Perhaps the first image that comes to mind is an athletic superstar with a room full of first-place trophies. But we are not talking about a superstar performer. The champion we are referring to is "one who fights on behalf of another."[29] The champion of a cause is the person who steps up to defend and promote that cause, using everything within his or her power to make sure the cause succeeds.

An idea is worth nothing if it has no champion.

If you want the HOT Plan to succeed in your company, your program needs a HOT Champion. A HOT Champion is the administrator who directs all the moving parts of your program. Without this critical player on your team, it would be hard for the HOT Plan to function successfully.

The HOT Champion is the program director and therefore must be a person who understands the big picture of your company and is able to keep it in focus while staying on top of the many moving pieces of the HOT Plan program. It is the champion who acts as a day-to-day guardian for your HOT Plan. The HOT Champion tracks goals and points, modifies deadlines, updates information, and prepares monthly reports. The HOT Plan requires this type of consistent effort from one central person to keep processes flowing smoothly. It may surprise you, but it is the detail-oriented HOT Champion that, more than any other person, will be responsible for your HOT Plan's success.

The Big Picture

The first and most important characteristic of a HOT Champion is an ability to see the big picture. As program director, the HOT Champion will be called upon often to explain and clarify the Must Win Challenges (MWCs) and Key Initiatives (KIs) of the company to those who are writing HOT Targets (HOTs) and will also be part of the team that evaluates whether proposed targets are acceptable or need revision. But fluency with the MWCs and KIs is only one part of the big picture. A thorough understanding of the workings of the organization is also valuable.

The HOT Champion's Responsibilities

1 *Communication* of clear and consistent expectations to the members of the organization

2 *Oversight* of the mechanical aspects of the program

3 *Publishing*: awarding and denying points, updating HOTs, evaluating progress, celebrating successes

The HOT Champion must be someone who understands how each department and team in your company fits into the grand scheme of things. He or she must know each team's function, their recurring projects, and how projects tend to flow among different parts of your organization. The HOT Champion also must have a realistic grasp of project timelines – how long specific projects tend to take and common holdups in workflow that can cause goals to be delayed.

We resisted the idea of placing this much responsibility in the hands of one person when we first began the HOT Plan but soon discovered that the administration of the plan simply works best when it is coordinated by one person who has a comprehensive viewpoint of the organization. Finding an employee who is able to evaluate your company from this vantage point might sound like a tall order, but most organizations have at least one administrative member whose position gives him or her this overview. If there is no one available at your company to fulfill this role, prospective HOT Champions will need some time to educate themselves about your organization and gain a comprehensive perspective.

The HOT Champion also must see the big picture of how the MWCs, KIs, and HOTs flow between departments and teams. Some KIs require the coordination of several departments, with individual HOTs that must be coordinated in order to meet the larger deadlines. Other HOTs that arise from differing teams seem to duplicate each other, and this has to be addressed. This is best caught by one set of eyes reviewing all the goals.

A HOT Champion's Key Traits

1 Administrative-level perspective

2 Detail oriented and numbers savvy

3 Ability to communicate efficiently and humanely

4 Has no conflict of interest

5 Strong grasp of vision

If your business employs 500 or fewer people and your work is carried out in one geographic area, one HOT Champion is ideal. But if your company has more than 500 employees and is spread across multiple states or countries, it wouldn't be possible for one person to keep track of it all. Large, complex organizations require more complex solutions. If your organization has more than 500 employees, I suggest appointing one HOT Champion per division of 500 or fewer employees.

If you have multiple HOT Champions, however, add another layer of communication in order to coordinate their efforts.

In terms of time commitment, our Pitsco HOT Champion, Lisa, spends an average of two to three hours per week to coordinate the HOT Plan administration for around 200 employees. Lisa estimates that the workload for 500 employees would average closer to four hours a week in administrative time.

Obviously, this is a job for a natural-born organizer. Keep this in mind when selecting your HOT Champion. Lisa is an ideal choice for Pitsco because she is like a fish to water when it comes to details and organization and is highly tuned in to numbers and data. She is also knowledgeable and passionate about Pitsco. Her current position as company president grants her neutrality; she is not a member of any particular department or team for which she is reviewing and approving goals. This eliminates conflict of interest and increases her credibility with all teams across the organization. She is able to arbitrate disputes that come up between departments as necessary. When HOT Points, personal accountability, and bonus money all are at stake, the perception of impartiality in the HOT Champion becomes extremely important.

Reviewing and Approving Targets

Imagine that you've been chosen as the HOT Champion for your organization. In this role, you and your leadership team have communicated the vision, MWCs, and KIs at company meetings and in company communications. You've issued a deadline for HOTs and now they are pouring in from every corner of the company. The targets are sitting in your email inbox or in the *HOTware*™ database. There are hundreds – perhaps even thousands – of them, all waiting for you to read and give your *yea* or *nay*. What now?

It sounds like a daunting task. Particularly in a diverse company with a large number of employees, this mountain of targets can feel a little dizzying. But keeping a few tips in mind makes the process much more manageable.

We recommend these 12 tips to assist HOT Champions in the goal review process:

1. Discuss the HOTs with team leaders as they are being written, before the targets are submitted to you.

Prevention is the best medicine. If you can head off problems by speaking with your employees about target ideas and expectations during the phase when HOTs are being written, this can save everyone a lot of time and hair pulling later. Discussing these ideas doesn't mean going through every HOT they plan to write, but encourage your supervisors and team leaders to come to you with questions or unusual target ideas in advance.

2. Read the HOTs as one collection.

It might not be standard beach or bedtime reading material, but your company's list of HOTs will be the size of a small book by the time it is compiled. Even though you can read the individual targets as they trickle in over a span of time, if you only read here and there, you may forget the details. There likely will be many interconnections between targets of differing departments and teams. You'll get the big picture more easily if you review them comprehensively.

3. Keep the WWWH criteria in mind when reviewing HOTs.

It bears repeating: All HOTs must answer the four questions: **Who** is going to do **What** by **When**, and **How** will success be evidenced? That sounds like a lot to keep in mind when you are reviewing hundreds of targets. It is. But after you have developed an ability to think along these lines, it becomes second nature to size up a target according to the WWWH criteria. Gauging these attributes for a given target will at times require some knowledge of the personalities responsible for completing it.

4. Trust the judgment of supervisors who have been in their roles for several years. Scrutinize targets more closely that are submitted by less-experienced supervisors.

Supervisors who have been at their jobs for several years probably already have a good sense of the projects their teams will be handling, the length of time it takes to complete them, and any particular stressors that accompany them. Also, experienced supervisors are more realistic about what to expect from team members. By comparison, newer supervisors don't know their teams that well yet. Their HOTs are more likely to be full of guesswork. This is especially true for new departments and teams. In the case of less-experienced supervisors and team leaders, the HOT Champion must allow more time to evaluate the targets they submit and give guidance as to how many hours the HOTs will take to accomplish.

Trust the judgment of supervisors who have been in their roles for several years.

5. Trust your supervisors.

No matter what the system is, there is always the potential for someone to try to cheat it. When points and money are involved, the fear of someone taking advantage of your company can become urgent. In reality, few people will be predisposed to approach the system in the spirit of evading responsibility if the culture of your organization stresses responsibility. Those who would look to manipulate the system will be naturally constrained by the fact that HOTs are written by teams. Unless you have good reason to doubt an individual or a team, it is best to assume that people are acting in good faith. Any effort to game the system will be pretty simple to spot as you develop your eagle eye for inflated time sheets, and so on.

6. Require ambition.

Human nature being what it is, some sets of HOTs may not be ambitious enough to be considered legitimate. Requiring departments to submit at least one Above-and-Beyond HOT will go a long way toward heading this problem off, but you'll still need to keep your radar tuned for lackluster HOTs. Although some teams with underwhelming goals may try to slip under the radar, others create low targets on purpose because they lack confidence in their ability to reach more demanding goals. It may sound counter-intuitive, but the best way to build confidence in the insecure teams is to encourage them to be more ambitious. The team members might look a little queasy at first, but as their team racks up successes, they will thank you.

7. Watch for overly ambitious goals.

Conversely, there are the overachievers. Every now and again, one team will put all their eggs in one basket by piling too much work on a single HOT. Their collective heart is in the right place and certainly the high number of points they capture will be nice if they complete the target by the deadline. But it is risky to make projects too large; if the HOT Target deadline isn't met, the team will fail to make any points at all or at best will gain only half. When you sense that a team is piling too much work on one HOT, help them consider chunking the target into smaller pieces. That way, credit can be awarded for work as the chunks are completed and turned in, moving step-by-step toward the completion of the larger project. This is a key strategy to helping your employees see success along the way as they achieve more complex HOTs.

8. When estimating the hours required to complete new projects, reference similar projects completed in the past.

When supervisors come to you shrugging because they have a new project but little idea how to gauge how much work will be required to see it through, a good question to ask would be "Is there another project your team has completed that you think this one might be like?" It is a simple question, one they might even have already asked themselves, but sometimes being asked directly by the HOT Champion helps focus the team leader's mind.

9. Watch for goals that might burden other teams.

If you notice that a team has declared a HOT that will depend on a substantial amount of work from another team, check the latter team's goals to make sure they have the same HOT included in their plan. If not, the first team might never have notified the other team that they would need their participation. As you can imagine, this could lead to some friction during the course of the year. With a little experience, it is easy to spot this potential issue in the early stages. Through the HOT review process, you can actually minimize this type of trouble for your organization in the coming year.

10. Watch for goals that aren't in the service of the organization.

HOTs can be noble, suitably ambitious, and well written, but if they don't support the MWCs, KIs, or the culture of your organization, they do not belong in the list of approved HOTs. The connection between the HOT and the MWC, KI, or culture of the company needs to be very clear. Sometimes, teams produce targets flawed in this particular manner because they are attempting to try something innovative. An innovative spirit is to be commended, but an irrelevant target must be reworked to line up with the direction of the company that has been set by the executive team through the MWCs and KIs.

> *HOT Targets must align with the Must Win Challenges and Key Initiatives.*

11. Take the time to explain why a HOT is being rejected.

This brings to light another function of the HOT Champion: arbitrating the rejection of proposed HOTs. Arbitration of a target's rejection is best approached by seeking the reason the target was misaligned. Perhaps the team simply is confused on the meaning of the MWCs and needs more clarity. If so, this can be a great teachable moment.

Be prepared to allow enough time to process this with the team leader. Sometimes, an explanation can be handled in just a few words. But other times, a cursory comment will not be enough. If supervisors don't clearly understand some piece of the goal-creation puzzle, they may never have that lightbulb moment unless the HOT Champion takes time to explore with them why and where they have erred. In the end, it will save a lot of time and enhance a positive company culture to get this confusion cleared up as soon as possible.

12. Creating great HOTs gets easier.

If you make mistakes, rest assured that the system won't break. For both the HOT Champion and your organization, the first year of the HOT Plan is likely to be a little wobbly. The first year Pitsco ran its HOT Plan, only about 50 percent of the goals were completed. People didn't totally understand the process and had not yet developed the mind-set of vigilance needed to stay on top of the program's processes. But by the second year, we added many percentage points in our completion rate and have been on a generally upward trend ever since. We now declare over 1,000 targets and the target completion/reportage rate crests annually at around 90 percent. A bumpy start is just part of the process. Don't be discouraged.

Tracking Target Completion

As teams come to their HOT Target due dates, most will submit their completed HOTs and eagerly await the HOT Champion's approval and the acknowledgment of the points they've earned. But sometimes midstream surprises come into play and the team gets behind. Getting behind on work will prompt requests for target alterations or deadline changes. Reports of completed targets or requests for extended deadlines trickle in steadily throughout the year, and it takes no great effort to keep up with the record keeping for these changes if the HOT Champion stays on top of it. But little tasks like these pile up quickly if not immediately attended to. Once a month is not an adequate check-in for updating target completion or requests for lengthened deadlines. Taking care of this business at least once or twice a week is a necessity.

> *Faith in the accuracy of the HOT Target road map begins to erode if progress is not updated regularly.*

It is important to remember that the completion of HOTs creates the road map of your year. Employees frequently look at completed HOTs as a gauge of their collective success. At Pitsco, if we fall even a little behind in keeping Pitsco's target tallies up to date, we hear comments about it from our employees! Employees' faith in the accuracy of the map erodes quickly if you fall behind in awarding points for completed HOTs. But when you keep on top of HOT Points, confidence grows because everyone in the company can plainly see the progress and celebrate great moments together.

Of course, a credible reporting of HOTs also reveals when progress isn't being made; setbacks are visible as well. This is also good for the company. It increases transparency and teamwork.

Many organizations tout their internal transparency and sing the praises of its effects, but true transparency cannot be achieved without a system. The HOT Plan provides a system that creates transparency across all levels. As the HOT Champion posts updates to completed HOTs, clarity is increased. That clarity is lost if the HOT Champion can't keep up with the work.

Adjusting HOTs and Updating Deadlines

Throughout the year, leadership will need to adjust HOTs, regardless of how much time and effort goes into planning them. Teams are encouraged to request needed changes from the HOT Champion. If your experience is like ours, the majority of the requests will be for additional time in completing HOTs, but some may come simply because the HOT wasn't well conceived or because circumstances changed. We have three rules of thumb in responding to requests.

1. **Modifications can't be requested after the due date.** If a team missed its deadline without notifying the HOT Champion, we make no alterations.

2. **A target may be altered only twice.** This goes for both the aim of the target and for the deadline. The reason is obvious: unlimited changes would strip accountability from the system.

3. **A proposed new date still must match the work required to complete the goal in question.** That is to say, teams should not just push their deadlines as far away from the present as possible just to put off dealing with the goal. The new deadline proposed should allow time to make up for the delay yet still provide healthy pressure to complete the work efficiently.

True transparency cannot be achieved without a system.

Special Cases

Learn to expect special cases and deal with them individually as they arise. A HOT Champion must be able to make solid decisions and stand by them. It is not possible to anticipate each individual situation that will come up while administering a 12-month HOT Plan. A good rule of thumb is to handle unanticipated situations as congruently as possible with the MWCs, the KIs, and the culture of your company. Some things eventually will require clarification through creating a new rule, but most can be decided quickly without the need for new policy.

Awarding Partial Points

For goals related to revenue, if we must award only partial points, we generally award a number of points equal to the percentage achieved at the time of the deadline. If a team has a goal to bring in $100,000 and they only bring in $90,000, we give them 90 percent of the points, rounded as closely as possible. Again, the money that was raised represents hard work on the part of those employees, so we believe it is too harsh to totally shut the team out on points simply because they did not make 100 percent of their goal.

For HOTs not related to revenue, we have a different policy. As long as a HOT is worth at least three points, we award half points for a late target completed within two weeks of its deadline. If a goal worth four points is due February 1 and the team doesn't complete it until February 14, we'll award two points. Why do we do this? Our reasoning is simple: we don't want teams to give up on a target they have poured themselves into; there should be some points awarded for all of their hard work. Let there be a moderate repercussion for missing deadlines, but make the focus on helping teams taste success whenever possible.

This forgiving spirit could go a little too far, though. HOT Teams have two weeks to earn half points and not a day more. If that same team with the February 1 deadline ended up completing their target on February 15, no points would be earned.

Pitsco is not so merciful when teams simply fail to make any communication attempts before a goal's deadline. If there are no attempts made at communication when a supervisor sees a HOT is in trouble – no completion notices, no requests for deadline extensions – the HOT Champion assumes that the supervisor was simply not mindful of the deadline. In this situation, no points are awarded. This policy encourages supervisors to continually stay in touch with Tribal and make use of the built-in accountability system.

No doubt there will be unique situations in your organization that demand unique solutions. However, the takeaway here is that awarding points doesn't have to be an all-or-nothing proposition.

Publishing Progress

At Pitsco, we publish the collective progress of our HOT Teams in several different ways. We print a table of all the points in our employee newsletter. We regularly add news items to our employee intranet about the progress that teams are making, and we celebrate successes at employee meetings. Of course, there is always an up-to-the-minute list of all the goals and points available to every employee via the *HOTware* database.

Keeping employees updated on regular progress builds momentum.

The table we print lists all the teams and then gives the up-to-date numbers in the following categories:

- Number of goals
- Points assigned
- Points earned
- Points lost
- Totals for each division and grand totals for the whole organization

Celebrating Your Story

The story of your organization's year is largely told in the hitting and missing of HOTs. All the effort you pour into the program is done to ensure that your story has the happiest ending possible. And although a successful finish will be cause for celebration at the end of the year, there is no reason to save all the jubilation for the annual HOT Check party. Getting the word out about the successes that your teams create regularly enables your company to celebrate all along the way.

At Pitsco, we love to celebrate, both as a whole company and among the departments and teams. Word even gets out in our community that we're a celebrating sort of company. Not long ago, one of my employees told me she was chatting with her siblings about some party preparations she was involved in for work. Her brother rolled his eyes and exhaled.

"We all know about you and your endless string of celebrations at the office," he said. "Is that all you guys do at Pitsco? Some of us actually have to work for a living!"

We do plenty of work,
but we also celebrate that work.

We loved it when we heard this. It's true, we love a party. Accomplishing our HOTs gives us lots to party about! Increase the joy in your workplace by using the HOT Plan and set up a culture of celebration.

Chapter Eleven

HOT Coaches

E very team needs a coach and HOT Teams are no exception.
In the HOT Plan, supervisors are the coaches of their teams. According to legendary Dallas Cowboys coach Tom Landry, teams who win require more than talent.

"The secret to winning," Landry said, "is constant, consistent management."[30]

Three Pitsco supervisors who provide constant, consistent management for their HOT Teams are Nancy, Tim, and Tom. Though the departments they supervise differ greatly, their jobs as supervisors share a common focus: to motivate, inspire, and lead their teams to success.

> ## *"The secret to winning is constant, consistent management."*
> ## *– Tom Landry*

Nancy joined the Pitsco family 24 years ago as a secretary and has ascended through numerous roles to her current position as director of educator insights. She now leads a team that analyzes market trends, conducts focus groups, interprets qualitative and quantitative data from customers, and collects internal information through employee questionnaires and surveys. She is also the team recorder for Tribal Council and the team leader for a HOT Team.

Tim joined Pitsco 24 years ago as an employee in the Synergistic warehouse and is now the machine shop and plastics assistant supervisor – a small, tightly focused division of Pitsco that acts as a short-run production company for curriculum product orders. Tim coordinates the workflow of the machine shop, watches over the HOT Targets (HOTs), and invents better ways to make products regularly. He works alongside his employees both as a supervisor and as a mentor, seeking to help them grow as machinists as they partner to produce the products needed by students who use the Pitsco curriculum modules.

Tom joined Pitsco 18 years ago to edit curriculum and has served in numerous writing, coding, and publication capacities throughout the company. As communications manager, Tom now supervises all Pitsco publications, grant funding research, the Editing Department and Media Relations. He oversees Pitsco's four external publications – the *Pitsco Network* magazine and three newsletters: *Rising Stars*, *Global Pitsco Network*, and *SySTEM Alert!* – along with an internal newsletter, the *Pit Stop*. He also oversees the content for the company intranet pipeline. He serves as captain of one HOT Team, cocaptain of another, and recorder on a third team.

The Right Person for the Job

What are the qualities of a good HOT Team leader or supervisor?

If you ask Nancy, her usual reply is that she considers what kind of boss she would like for her son to have. Her son is still in his 20s and just starting his career life. She aspires to be that kind of supervisor to others.

Supervisors transmit your company's culture and values.

If you ask Tim, he will tell you that being the best supervisor in the machine shop means being a hands-on leader.

"I don't feel like I am the typical supervisor," Tim says. "I am a working supervisor; I work alongside my guys. Since my mentor and former department head, Frank, retired, I have the most experience as a machinist in our shop. Now it is up to me to mentor the others."

If you ask Tom, one of the primary qualities of a good communications supervisor is coordinating the information flow to optimize the team's success.

"It's critical for the supervisor to get input from everyone on the team when creating the HOT goals (HOTs)," Tom says. "The supervisor must also help define roles and make sure employees are working in the role best suited for them."

> ## To lead winning teams, supervisors must be able to cultivate potential.

From my position as a CEO, I've come to understand that excellent supervisors have many traits in common, but those traits that help them facilitate employee ownership of responsibility within the context of the HOTs are the ones most critical to the success of the HOT Plan. It is critical to cultivate your company's supervisors because the supervisors are the one-on-one transmitters of your company culture and values.

To lead winning teams, HOT Plan supervisors must be observant, target driven, able to cultivate the potential of each member of the group, and able to understand and communicate the company vision.

Observant

Good supervisors see the whole painting but don't necessarily notice the details and the brush strokes – until they need to. Though oriented to taking in the big picture in their management vision, supervisors still must be capable of looking deeply at a particular issue when called upon to do so. This ability to zoom in when necessary is a by-product of a continual study of the general environment and, simply put, requires a supervisor to intentionally and thoughtfully observe the people who work for him or her.

A good understanding of the people inside a department equips a supervisor to see into the true nature of any issues that arise. Most problems are people problems. That isn't necessarily negative; it is often just the case that different people need different things in order to be successful.

"When you have dialogues with your employees," Nancy says, "they will tell you all sorts of things even if you don't ask them directly. If you just listen to the things people say, you will hear what's important to them and know what each employee needs to be truly successful. As a supervisor, when you have the latitude, you allow them whatever it is that they need to help them do their best in their job."

> *"... just listen to the things people say, you will ... know what each employee needs to be truly successful."*
> *— Nancy, director of educator insights*

Nancy relates the skill of careful observation of the personality differences on your team to lessons she learned while raising her own children.

"As my kids were growing up, one was very definitely an athlete and the other one was a singer," she says. "So I had the athlete and the artist — two different personalities. We realized this even when they were young and tried to provide for them as individuals. Sometimes, she would say, 'That's not fair. He got this and I didn't,' or he would say, 'She got to do that and I didn't get to do it.' I replied that as parents, it's our responsibility to make sure our children have what they need, but these are not necessarily the same things. You might need one thing to be successful, but she needs something different. As a boss, it's a similar process."

This type of flexibility based on observant leadership was recently illustrated in Nancy's department. The group was reading and discussing a particular book together as part of their HOTs, but Nancy soon realized that one person in the group hated to read while another employee who loved to read was struggling to keep up because of a particularly high volume of work at the time. To keep the exercise enjoyable and rewarding for these two team members, she provided a CliffsNotes version of the book for both. Some might criticize the fact that some employees have to read the entire book while others are allowed a CliffsNotes version. But Nancy knew that reading every word of the original volume was never the point of the HOT. The point of the goal was personal growth and deepening team bonds through the book discussions.

Target Driven

Writing HOTs might come naturally to some, but it does not always come easily for others. Supervisors must keep this in mind and work to keep the entire team on board as they develop their HOTs. Tim uses a monthly list of targets to keep his team on track.

"In addition to our shop's annual targets, I print out a list of monthly targets based on the work orders that have come in at the first of each month and it becomes the basis of our monthly targets," Tim says. "Our intention is to finish the entire list by the end of the month."

Good supervisors see the relationship between an individual target and the endgame.

A supervisor is in a natural position to set an attitude of timeliness such as this in completing the HOTs. The whole team will internalize this mind-set if supervisors are goal-driven, keeping an eye toward deadlines and issuing reminders. The Plastics Department of the machine shop is a good example of a team that keeps timeliness as a priority.

"If plastics has a back order, we have a HOT Target that says it must be turned around within 48 hours," Tim says. "If we meet that standard for an entire year, we capture substantial points."

The good news is that the department has met this goal four years in a row.

A supervisor who does not make targets a priority as Tim did, however, or adopts a lackluster posture toward hitting targets will not inspire above-and-beyond aspirations in his or her department. Not all targets are fun; of course, some are just plain old work. That much is a given. But good supervisors see the relationship between an individual target and the endgame and keep their team encouraged and driven to meet their goals.

Cultivate the Potential of Each Member of the Group

In the framework of the HOT Plan, cultivating the potential of each member of the team begins with getting all members to help in the goal-creation process. As a supervisor, it is difficult to keep the voices of the group balanced and open to all because some members of the group naturally are more outgoing and speak up more than others. The outgoing ones are not shy to share their views during HOT brainstorming times. Yet the most reticent people in the room often have given much thought to their ideas and are an invaluable resource. How can these quieter members of the team be encouraged to speak up?

One way supervisors get full participation of all members of the team is to provide a structure for participation that helps those who are more reticent to prepare for sharing. Nancy requests that team members come to the planning sessions with a list of goals in hand. By requesting this, Nancy provides a way for the more reserved members of the team to have space to develop their thoughts in solitude. Prewritten goals have guidelines – they are based on what worked (or didn't work) in the previous year. There is also room for new ideas. When it is time for the meeting, everyone comes prepared to share their lists and none are overlooked.

Getting full input from every team member is a top priority for Tom.

"At the end of the year, everybody gets the opportunity to participate in developing the HOTs," Tom says. "Within our department, looking at the list of goals, you can find every single person represented multiple times. I think that is why our team is strong on completing their HOTs; they don't ever just quit on their goals as the year goes on. They all have a stake in it."

Tom believes the HOT Plan creates a natural process that helps him play to the strengths of his employees. To get the most out of your employees, he advises supervisors or team leaders to be realistic about what they can and can't do.

> *"To get the most out of your employees, you have to be realistic about what they can and can't do."*
> *– Tom, communications manager*

"The HOT Plan helps supervisors analyze whether they have the right employees in the right spots," he points out. "In order to be successful with the plan, your employees have to be successful with their individual responsibilities. If they are not well-suited to the tasks assigned to them, then you want to change things around so they can be successful."

The HOT Plan is most effective in departments where the supervisor and employees sit down as a team, discuss projects and anticipated workload, and then establish goals in concert with one another. The HOT Plan is much less effective in departments where the supervisor completes this process solo.

Understand the Company Vision

Of course, the supervisor must have a clear sense of the company vision and must be able to communicate it.

"It's your job as a supervisor to know the vision, the KIs, the MWCs," Tom says. "Tribal Council does a great job sharing the info with everyone, but getting it out to every department involves a trickle-down effect that depends on the supervisors."

For Tim, vision begins with a very concrete image: kids in classrooms that need the products he is building to do their lessons.

"I can't write curriculum; I wouldn't even know where to begin," Tim says. "But if the kids we are preparing these products for do not have to wait for them past deadline, that's my biggest contribution to the vision."

When it comes to vision, Nancy's focus also centers on the kids helped by Pitsco. For Nancy, this focus stems from a personal experience with a particular student.

"In my mind, I go back to a classroom I visited in North Carolina where there's a little boy sitting on the floor," Nancy recalls. "His teacher pointed him out to me and told me he was a year older than his peers and had always struggled with his schoolwork. But the new Pitsco product they were using fit his learning style and he quickly became a leader; suddenly, he was the one the other kids turned to for help – even the smart kids. For the first time in his life, he was the star. It changed everything for him. That's what drives me, that picture in my mind of a little boy being given a chance to succeed."

I've seen tears come to Nancy's eyes when she tells this story. A supervisor with an emotional connection to your company's vision will not only work hard to fulfill it, he or she will infect others on the team with that same passion.

The HOT Plan: A Supervisor's Toolkit

What the HOT Plan does for a company, it can also do in miniature for a supervisor or team leader.

Although leadership theory has moved on from envisioning supervisors as taskmasters who treat those below them as blocks to be moved around, in reality, this is still the way many supervisors handle human management. They probably don't do this because they are cynical or because they don't sense there is a better way, but they lack a clear procedure for taking the high road and under pressure revert to their default mode.

> *What the HOT Plan does for a company, it can do in miniature for a supervisor or team leader.*

The HOT Plan supplies a better system. If supervisors and team leaders apply themselves to learning the system and are willing to adjust their frame of reference, they will find that HOTs are a great resource for harnessing the creativity of all their workers, spurring independent action, directing workflow, and emphasizing the importance of getting things done in a timely manner. The HOT Plan can be the procedural paradigm shift that helps them become the kinds of leaders that modern business theory always lauds.

But old ways of thinking die hard. I chose my words carefully when I said that many would have to change their approach. There might be some resistance at first, as I experienced during those first lackluster years with the HOT Plan. The fact is, I could have done more to show that I was serious about the HOT Plan and that I was serious about empowering them.

Our work in education reform parallels this paradigm shift in business.

For thousands of years, teachers stood before their pupils and pontificated about their knowledge. The student was viewed as an empty vessel to be filled with the teacher's information – in whatever manner the teacher thought best.

Pitsco was not the only voice, nor the first, to speak up and say that the old model needed some revision. But we certainly were early to the conversation in the education market. We pointed out that individual student creativity and curiosity needed to be the driver of education, not a teacher-led, lecture-based model. Instead of lecture, the teacher's role should be to harness students' curiosity, creativity, and natural desire to learn. To prove this, we created curriculum called Modules that gave students the tools to work in a self-directed manner. Our education Modules took the teacher off the stage and put him or her in the midst of the students, directing their learning as needed.

Many teachers immediately fell in love with the Modules system, but some resisted, perceiving the modules as added work and loss of power for the teacher. But education Modules grant power and responsibility instead of reducing it, just like the workout instructions on individualized 3" x 5" cards that I handed to my Weleetka track team. Though there is a small learning curve for writing HOTs, the system ultimately streamlines processes for supervisors just as the Modules did for teachers and the workout cards did for me as a coach. The HOT Plan offers many advantages to supervisors, management, and team leaders.

A Clear Plan for Everyone

The clarity that the HOT Plan provides increases the effectiveness of supervisors, according to Nancy.

"The HOT Plan allows me to plan the work that my team will do," she told me. "The projects and deadlines are laid out for the year, so everyone knows what we're going to be doing. I don't care if my people work on their current project in the morning or the afternoon, it just needs to get done. It's a great way to structure an employee's work without me constantly saying, 'Do this now, do that now, and do this now.' They create a plan and they go work it."

> *"[HOTs are] a great way to structure an employee's work."*
> *– Nancy, director of educator insights*

Everyone has access to their written goals. At Pitsco, we make them available to all employees through a database. But Nancy, as well as several others who supervise with *HOTware*™, takes it a step further. Nancy has one-on-one meetings once a month or so with each of the workers in her department. These meetings usually last 30 minutes to an hour. When they step into her office to discuss their projects, she opens up the database and pulls up the HOTs. They look at what the team already has accomplished and what is coming up. They discuss whether they are on track to finish their work toward a goal. If not, is there anything she can do to assist them? Or perhaps the plan needs to be adjusted and the goal updated.

For the most part, work stays on track. Long-term projects require a mix of solo work and cooperative effort, and when the latter is needed, they orchestrate it themselves, which is an expectation that Nancy cultivates. It isn't that her employees don't need a little push now and again, but the onus for figuring out how to reach completion in their part of the puzzle is on them. If, despite everyone's best efforts, the group won't be meeting one of their deadlines, requesting changes is a painless procedure. The policy of allowing up to two changes per HOT demonstrates that the HOT Plan is flexible when it needs to be. At the same time, it is not so flexible that groups lose the imperative to get work done. After all, there is no shortage of work to do.

It is inevitable that there will be crunch times and that occasionally a team will feel one of their targets breathing down their neck. This is minimized by the kind of frequent consultation of the goals that Nancy and her team do, and that is one of the secrets of success. Our *HOTware* database also notifies supervisors and team leaders by email when a deadline is approaching (a courtesy of the system), but supervisors shouldn't wait until this reminder to begin considering a goal.

The HOTware™ *database notifies supervisors/team leaders when a deadline is approaching.*

And similarly, though a supervisor shouldn't be continually telling her workers what to do next, she will remind them what deadlines are on the horizon. In particular, this ensures that Above-and-Beyond HOTs aren't a disruption to normal workflow. A supervisor in a manufacturing setting, for example, oversees a lot of work with no clear stopping points in production. Without appropriate foresight, a looming deadline for a HOT that is outside the scope of this work might be a disruption.

Tom looks to HOTs to provide a clear plan for everyone in his department; he also uses the HOTs as a tool of motivation.

"The HOTs provide a sense of purpose and focus," Tom says. "Focus is the main thing; everyone in the department knows what the primary goals are. And for every project they are involved with, they know what their role is and it is posted for everybody to see."

The Company Has Your Back

It is a common story at some organizations: a supervisor with a brilliant idea he is itching to try submits the idea through a traditional company hierarchy and waits for it to work its way up to someone who can give the final OK to the idea. During the process, the supervisor grows accustomed to wishy-washy, tentative enthusiasm. Finally, if he is lucky, he gets the OK to go forward with the idea. But when the time actually comes to put it into practice, the company pulls the rug out from under him by balking at something at the last minute (usually expenses) or by implementing a different new idea instead. The supervisor is left to wonder why he is even there at all if the company doesn't value their ideas.

This is so typical that most supervisors who are reading this chapter could complete the above story line with names, faces, and details. Not with the HOT Plan, however. If you are a supervisor in a HOT Plan company, the outcome is different. The company wants your input and has your back.

If you are a supervisor in a HOT Plan company, the company wants your input and has your back.

Tim always closely observes the processes in his area in order to identify ways to increase efficiency. When he or his team comes up with a new idea they want to try, Tim gets excited. By declaring it as a HOT, Tim knows he will receive the needed support from the company for his group's idea. The company might not always approve the submitted goal, but if the company approves, the company lends its full support to the idea, which includes financial resources and training. In this way, Tim believes, Pitsco gives groups a chance to zero in on things they need to accomplish during the year by submitting them as HOTs.

The HOT Plan not only benefits the company but also lends support to everyone in the organization. It serves as a contract with all parties, helping them get on the same page regarding expectations and commitments. The bond that a company, a supervisor, and his or her team forge over HOTs is a statement of faith in one another.

The Power of a Good Supervisor

The HOT Plan gives supervisors the leverage to be successful. Great supervisors multiply the strengths of the HOT Plan by ensuring that the team takes the MWCs, KIs, and HOTs seriously, uses them as guidelines for their work, and diligently monitors their progress.

> *CEOs, vice presidents, and top management must know their supervisors well.*

A word to the wise for CEOs and other top leadership in any company: know your supervisors well. When your company is small, chances are you will know everyone personally. But once your company grows past 100 employees, this is no longer possible. Transferring the locus of responsibility is the key to your company's future success. It is the supervisors who are the key to this transfer. It is important to have complete buy-in among supervisors through dedicated training in supervisor development meetings or other training opportunities.

Supervisors don't just manage people – they sit at the hub of influence in your company. Supervisors are on the front lines of communicating your vision and your strategic initiatives (the MWCs and KIs) and transferring the locus of responsibility to employees. Know – and take care of – your supervisors.

Chapter Twelve

HOT Leaders

E very person is endowed with something special and unique to give to the world.

Not everyone believes this or recognizes their own gift. There are many who do not fully develop their gift or allow themselves to follow their gift, wherever it leads. But in my experience, those who embrace their gift are happier in life and more empowered to affect the world in positive ways. Those who are willing to risk the journey – the journey to discover and use their gifts to better mankind – are leaders of the highest order. Yet this natural form of leadership may or may not have anything at all to do with their employment or their rank or position in society.

We have a phrase we sometimes use around Pitsco. We refer to ourselves as a *company of leaders*. It has a nice ring to it, you must admit. But honestly, what does the phrase really mean?

Leadership is about pushing beyond what is expected, caring about quality, and working with vision. These traits certainly are not the sole property of any particular personality type or position in a company. Leadership is not only found in C-staff positions, rousing speeches, and revolutionary ideas.

The HOT Plan encourages true leadership to grow by defining your company culture as one of responsibility and accountability. Such a culture attracts and cultivates the spirit of leadership among employees of all levels.

As a company, Pitsco has a gift to give students and teachers: *leading education that positively affects learners*. Through the use of HOT Targets (HOTs), employees influence how they give that gift. And as they hit their targets, they are joint leaders in giving Pitsco's gift.

The CEO and administrators of any complex, thriving business can't manage all the details of a company while simultaneously preserving the focus it takes to keep their corporation on track. That is why vision and leadership must be shared across the company by entrusting the locus of responsibility for work to those who are most directly responsible for the tasks.

A Culture of Responsibility

The HOT Plan at Pitsco serves the company, but it also serves those who work for it. The plan gives employees a voice, aids them in long-term planning, and fosters leadership skills.

What does a company culture look like when its employees are a company of leaders? I'd like to consider this by telling you three stories.

> *The HOT Plan at Pitsco serves the company, but it also serves those who work for it.*

Leaders and Creative Problem Solving

Recently, an innovative idea came out of the machine shop at Pitsco.

Pitsco manufactures maglev racers among hundreds of other products for students. The racers, just like vehicles powered by magnetic levitation in the real world, require a special track. For manufacture, each piece of aluminum track requires that five holes be punched at precise intervals. Because of limitations in the machinery, it used to be that these holes had to be drilled one at a time. This was time consuming and if the measurement was off, the piece was ruined.

Frank, a veteran machinist and supervisor of the shop for many years, and Tim, the current supervisor mentioned in the previous chapter, hatched a plan together.

Their plan was to modify an old punch press in the department into a machine that could punch all five holes in one go. There wasn't money to buy a new machine or to order new parts, so they had to retrofit the existing machine from old parts that were not being used in the shop. They added five cams on a single shaft to do the punching, metal guides, and guards in order to meet OSHA standards. For HOT Target purposes, this type of activity would be considered an Open HOT as a spontaneous solution or an Above-and-Beyond HOT if it had been planned.

> *If employee initiative is truly*
> *valued by your organization,*
> *your people will innovate.*

The two men weren't sure their idea would work, and they didn't try to pretend they were. Every puncture the machine punches in the metal saps a little force from the strike, and they were banking on the fact that there was enough excess force to accommodate their modification. They had their fingers crossed, but they thought it was worth a try because of the potential benefit to production. After they made their modifications, they took the punch press for a spin. They placed a piece of the aluminum track into position and – *Ka-chunk* – it worked! After a few trials, they declared it a success. What once took 10 minutes now took about 30 seconds.

Because they took the initiative to solve a problem, the machine shop can now produce the track at a greater efficiency than it could previously – and Frank and Tim can take pride in their accomplishment. As a company, we trusted their expertise and their imagination, and it paid off. Great employees take charge of their own problem solving if given a system that allows them to do so.

If your organization truly values employee initiative, your people will sense it and feel free to innovate, to think outside of the box, and to come up with their own solutions. They will share these innovative ideas with their supervisor, something that takes a surprising amount of courage for many people. Some of the ideas shared by employees may seem implausible in the mind of a supervisor, but the supervisor should give all ideas fair consideration. Even if an idea doesn't work, it still is productive. It gives the supervisor an opportunity to explain why and build trust and to let employees know that speaking up is appreciated. Appreciation encourages creative problem solving. A treasury of good ideas for every company can be found among its employees as long as the culture supports them and a system is in place to harness their good ideas.

In terms of the HOT Plan, sharing great ideas is most effective during the target-declaration phase. But creativity can come from anywhere and at any time, and the principle really applies all year long. There have been numerous instances at Pitsco in which creative, employee-generated ideas led to great Open HOTs that were declared in the middle of the year.

The Passion to Serve

Patty, communications assistant at Pitsco, is the kind of worker who comes in early, stays late, and has her own key to the office. Patty takes on a large number of projects of her own initiative – from updating company style books to keeping the refrigerator clean in her office break room. Patty's passion to serve is part of who she is. It motivates her to give herself fully to whatever she does, including her company. She takes ownership of her work.

Writing HOTs increases that sense of ownership, according to Patty.

"As an employee, when I build my own project schedule and am given the opportunity to decide how to approach and accomplish my work, I feel a stronger connection to that work," she said. "The same thing happens on a broader scale with departments and teams."

Patty is a fan of letting cross-departmental teams collaborate on targets and believes the HOT Plan increases communication within the company.

"I think it is cool that what the HOT Plan accomplishes at a team level spreads across the organization and encourages collaboration between departments," she said.

*"When I am given the opportunity
to decide how to approach
and accomplish my work, I feel
a stronger connection to that work."
– Patty, communications assistant*

For people like Patty, there is another perk for employees when departments join forces: personal growth.

"Cross-departmental collaboration gives you a chance to learn different skills, to learn from other departments," Patty said. "When we were working with other teams to build the high school curricula, I learned how to navigate the computer games database and how the Quality Assurance Department tracks issues with their software. The opportunity to partner on HOT Targets opened my eyes to areas of the company I didn't even know existed and encouraged me to explore more."

True passion displays itself in many ways; it can be obvious or subtle. But one thing is clear: employees passionate about their work do more than meet minimum requirements. They look for ways to grow the company and to grow professionally at the same time. The HOT Plan mobilizes employee passion and gives an opportunity for engaged employees to shine.

Leaders and Organizational Impact

When Open HOTs were first made available to our employees, we struggled with getting teams to declare them. Even though they were doing work that could be declared under Open HOTs, employees failed to take credit for their work and were missing out on the points – and thus they were missing out on the bonus cash. This added up, collectively, to more than $16,000 left on the table – more than $80 per person – in the first year that Open HOTs were announced. Apparently, we hadn't promoted Open HOTs as strongly as we needed to. Dorcia, senior development specialist and project manager in our Sales Department, saw an opening to make a difference and became the leader in correcting this.

Because of the ways in which departments and teams are interlocked, the HOT Plan fosters a sense of how one's individual work affects the larger company.

As the next year went by, she kept her eye on the target totals and began firing off reminder emails to various supervisors about Open HOTs. Toward the end of the year, she even became something of a guru about Open HOTs. People throughout the company began coming to her with their questions about which projects could be claimed as Open HOTs. Her work paid off: Open HOTs began to be claimed at a much higher rate than before. Ultimately, that year became one of the biggest years ever for Pitsco's HOT Check, and it was the first time we completed over 90 percent of the declared HOTs. Dorcia made a difference. Her leadership had an immediate and obvious impact across the entire organization.

Because of the ways in which departments and teams are interlocked, the HOT Plan fosters a sense of how one's individual work affects the larger company. It becomes obvious that each person's work has a ripple effect when targets are hit or missed and points are won or lost. This heightened awareness of one's impact on others in the company increases willingness to lead and seems to be a natural side effect of the HOT Plan.

A Walk About Pitsco

On sunny days, I like to take a walk about the campus of our company and visit the different departments. It is satisfying to see the fruits of the HOT Plan as I watch our employees going about their projects. At first glance, things look much as they did before the days of the HOT Plan. People are in the middle of one work task or another, and we each stop for few moments to chat before we go our separate ways. That much has not changed. But there is a difference, and it's one that runs deeper than the particular day's concerns.

The difference at Pitsco today is not so much in the quality of our employees – we have always had good luck finding talented, driven employees. The difference is that those employees are empowered to take charge of their work as co-carriers of the vision.

In Research and Development, Gary and Paul are leaning over a worktable, putting the finishing touches on the prototype of a new product they plan to get out by the start of the school year for kids with an interest in technology.

In education services, Tammy is on the phone with a school administrator. Tammy has been reviewing the district's curriculum profile and has called to let the administrator know about professional development opportunities we could provide for the teachers in the district.

In my own building on campus, Tonya, our controller, is reviewing accounts payable for a possible discrepancy she has identified. Just down the hall, our travel coordinator Ashlee is on the phone with one of our sales reps and rapidly typing, trying to get him to his destination on time after an airport delay.

In the Call Center, where I walk a little more quietly, Steve, Fred, and others are taking call after call, finding solutions for teachers who have run into baffling issues with their robotics equipment.

In the catalog graphics area, the dynamic duo Ben and Todd are putting the final shine on a volcano-themed product photo Todd set up and took in his own backyard.

In the Printed Media Center, Danielle and Sheila have just received a magazine proof and are checking it over for print issues.

In the warehouse, the picker/packers Jonathan, Jennifer, and others are pushing the clock to get through a list of items to ship by the end of the day.

I take a drive over to Manufacturing where I say hello to Tim and Jeff and admire the artistry of their machine work. From there, I step over to the final assembly area and visit with Brett and Gary as they assemble electronics components for an upcoming order. Gary tells me he is on a committee that will host a group of elementary students for a bottle rocket racer competition.

Employees work confidently when they see the connection between their handiwork and the overall vision of your company.

The work being done by all of these people in all of these departments is purposeful and efficient, honed through years of careful, honest observation with an eye on finding ways to do things better. Employees work confidently when they see and understand the connection between their own handiwork and the overall vision of our company.

The innovative insights of our employees, along with the passion and fearless ideas they bring to their tasks every day, continue to amaze me, but they no longer surprise me. This is what empowered employees look like. Standing among them, I know I am in the company of leaders. With a HOT Plan at work in your organization, you can be in the company of leaders too.

Part IV. HOT Stuff

Chapters

HOT Data

Most organizations have a watershed year or two in their history – a year that marks major changes in their organization's life.

The term *watershed year* derives from a geologic concept: the watershed divide, the place where the flow of water divides at a mountain ridgeline and follows a path to the lowest point in its landscape.[31] At the ridgeline, the flow of water divides distinctly; one side flows one direction, the other flows the other direction.

> *Everyone in the organization will remember the watershed year as the year when things changed.*

In business, the term *watershed year* describes a point in the company history that acts as a ridgeline. It is most easily recognized in hindsight. Company processes, procedures, and profitability before the watershed year flow one way, but after the watershed year, they flow another. Data and archived records of the company will all point back to the watershed year. Ultimately, everyone in the organization will remember the watershed year as the year when things changed.

When we examine the data that tells the story of Pitsco's success, 1997 stands out as our watershed year – the year we launched the HOT Plan. Company processes, procedures and profitability all flowed differently after 1997; in hindsight, it was clearly the year when things changed for the better. That is our story and we are excited to share it. But as excited as we are, we don't share our story just because we like to talk about it. We share it because we want it to be your story too.

We can say with confidence that the year your business adopts a HOT Plan will be the year things change for the better. Why can we be confident of this? Because when you change how things are done in any organization, you change the culture as well. Much more is happening to the organization than meets the eye.

A HOT Plan causes more change in an organization than meets the eye.

A British sociologist named Anthony Giddens codified this phenomenon into a communication theory in his book *The Constitution of Society* in 1984. He named the theory the Structuration Theory of Organizational Communication. Giddens said that organizational structure and culture do not exist separately from each other. Instead, the two forces are actively involved with each other; they are in fact cocreators.[32] When you change the structure, you affect the culture, and when you change the culture, you affect the structure.

To put Giddens' complex theory in very simple terms, organizational structure and culture are intertwined because organizational structure has to do with *how things get done* and culture has to do with the *attitudes with which people do them*. The two go hand in hand.

Changes in how things get done may seem minor at first, but in truth, even minor changes in how things get done cause a chain reaction in attitudes. What supervisor, teacher, or coach does not recognize this? To do things a new way, team members must cooperate, learn new things, work with different people, leave their comfort zones, and adopt new norms. The culture itself shifts to accommodate these changes.

Because the HOT Plan positively alters the way people plan, relate to, and accomplish their work, the first year of a successful HOT Plan sets in motion a positive change in the culture of your organization as well. As the HOT Plan increasingly empowers employees to influence how things get done, your organization's processes, procedures and profitability will begin to flow in a more team-based direction. This change will produce a watershed in your company's history – for the better.

Returning to the Pitsco story, 1997 was a year of many changes. In addition to launching the HOT Plan, Pitsco was involved with several other company firsts. Pitsco ventured into the high school market for the first time, introducing a curriculum called Pathways (later renamed Suites). Our groundbreaking Synergistic Systems curriculum was digitized for Internet delivery in 1997, multiplying its sales and effectiveness. Most significantly, Pitsco became the North American division for a well-known European educational products company in 1997. That move instantly expanded Pitsco's product line and markets dramatically. In order to efficiently handle the increased customer service demands, a major software upgrade was required. Consequently, we upgraded the entire software system for Pitsco customer service to the newest and sleekest 21st-century customer service management software available. To this day, all long-term customer service records begin in that watershed year, 1997.[33]

But the most powerful change occurring in 1997 was not the whirlwind of business expansion. Pitsco's most powerful change at that time was small and quiet, barely even noticeable; it was the fundamental shift in the company's culture. From the start, the HOT Plan exceeded its design as a motivational system for getting work done and became a culture shaper. The HOT Plan set in motion the highly engaged employee culture the company enjoys today. But why is employee engagement so important?

The Importance of Employee Engagement

Employee engagement continues to increase as a major concern for businesses around the world as they seek to integrate the complex and younger workforce emerging today. Research scholar Suresh Sirisetti defines the term *employee engagement* as "the means or strategy by which an organization seeks to build a true partnership between the organization and its employees." Indeed, it is increasingly recognized that this partnership is critical to employee retention, performance, and productivity.[34]

Employee engagement is evidence of a true partnership between an organization and its employees.

The 2012 Gallup survey of 1.4 million employees examined the impact of employee engagement on nine performance outcomes. Comparing the bottom quartile with the top quartile of highly engaged employees, the survey gives these figures:

- 37 percent lower absenteeism
- 25 percent lower turnover (in high-turnover organizations)
- 65 percent lower turnover (in low-turnover organizations)
- 48 percent fewer safety incidents
- 41 percent fewer quality incidents (defects)
- 10 percent higher customer metrics
- 21 percent higher productivity
- 22 percent higher profitability[35]

Sirisetti maintains that an engaged employee is one who is "intellectually and emotionally bound with the organization, feels passionately about its goals and is committed towards its values." This type of employee goes "the extra mile ... with the actions that drive the business."[36] With measurable performance outcomes directly tied to high employee engagement, business in the 21st century can no longer afford to look the other way when faced with the challenges of how to foster employee engagement.

In the first year of Pitsco's HOT Plan, employees were not highly engaged. Jane, a long-term employee who supervises a production area at Pitsco, remembers her doubts at the HOT Plan's beginnings.

"I thought maybe it would last five or 10 years then phase out and we would do something different," Jane recalls.

Employee teams generated 950 possible points in HOT Targets (HOTs) the first year the HOT Plan was implemented. By the end of that year, Pitsco's employees were proud to have attained 53 percent of those points, jointly collecting 503 points across the company. When those points were translated into dollars, every full-time employee pocketed a $92 bonus that year. The dollar amount may have been small, but the impact of the bonus on morale was big. The HOT Check was a confidence builder and gave incentive to employees to push the amount higher the next year. Still, I dreamed of the day that we might be able to pay out bonuses of $1,000 or more.

Highly engaged employee cultures perform better worldwide, across all economic classes.

Nearly 20 years later, my dream has come true, and then some. Employee buy-in to the HOT Plan is deeply embedded in the company's culture. Employees talk freely about not wanting to let fellow workers down by missing their HOT deadline. As mentioned in Chapter 8, HOTs permeate the very ethos of Pitsco. The HOT Plan has become "the way things are done" at Pitsco – a culture marker, according to researchers. The numbers easily track employee buy-in: By 2015, the number of HOT Points possible for the year had risen to 7,136. Pitsco employees collectively captured 91 percent of those points in 2015, or 6,503 points altogether. The resulting HOT Check based on those points reached an all-time high that year of approximately $1,800 per full-time employee, pretax.[37]

Embedded in the Culture

Just like the HOTs, the HOT Plan's values are now deeply embedded in Pitsco's culture. This is a critical step to creating a highly engaged workforce. In fact, according to Terry Irwin, founder and CEO of TCii Strategic and Management Consultants, real employee engagement is not possible unless it is embedded in the culture. The factors that drive high employee engagement, Irwin says, must be embedded in the organizational culture itself, or the employee engagement will not ultimately succeed.[38]

Since 1997, Pitsco's business landscape has completely changed. The business partnership that dramatically increased our product line has ended. New partnerships are being forged. Synergistic Systems was replaced with a newer curriculum, now known as Modules. In customer service, digital technology replaced that sleek 21st-century customer service software a while back. Profitability and sales now are driven by robotics and STEM (science, technology, engineering, and math) education. Pitsco's TETRIX Robotics lines – along with MATH and STEM *Expeditions* – help set Pitsco apart as a STEM education leader.

But in spite of all of these changes in the business landscape, one influence has remained the same: the HOT Plan.

Timeline Data

Through the years, the number of HOTs employees submit has continued to increase. The number of points set and attained continues to grow along with it, and the HOT Checks keep getting bigger.

But in addition to these internal measures of cultural success, an external measure – the number of students and teachers served by Pitsco's innovative educational product line – has also risen steadily.

HOT Points Possible vs HOT Points Attained

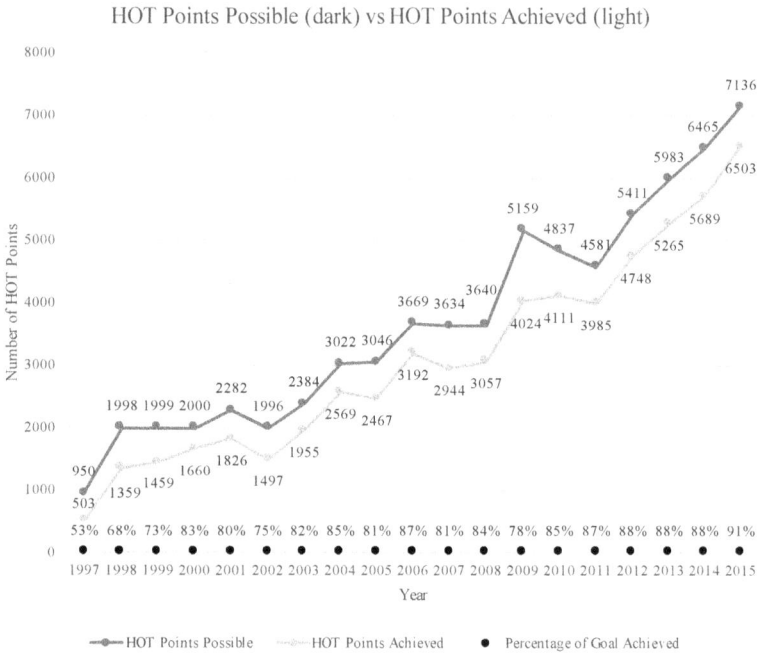

Chart 1: HOT Points Possible vs HOT Points Achieved, 1997-2015

When charted, the timeline data for Pitsco's HOT Plan history provides a picture of the steadily increasing employee buy-in over the years.

Timeline for HOT Check Growth

Chart 2: Pitsco HOT Check Bonus Growth, 2003-2015

Employees exercise real power over the amount of the bonus check by prioritizing HOTs and accomplishing them on time. Through the years, employees have developed a sense of camaraderie around the HOT Check amount. Many express an unwillingness to let their fellow employees down by missing a deadline and losing possible target points and the dollars they add to the overall company bonus. When deadlines are near, employees sometimes volunteer to work longer hours in order to meet them.

The HOT Plan and Return on Investment

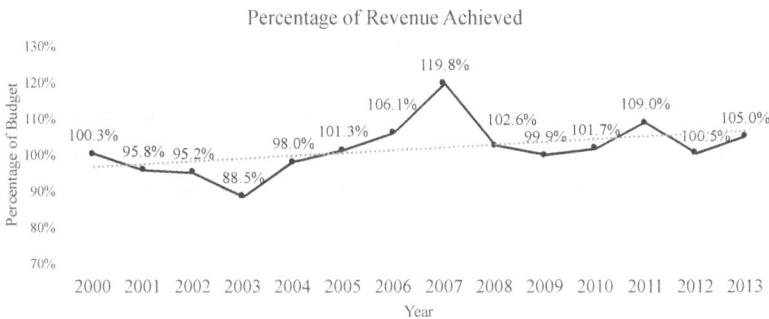

Chart 3: Percentage of Budget vs Percentage of Revenue Achieved, 2000-2013

How does the HOT Plan reflect in the bottom line of the company? Pitsco measures the financial impact of the HOT Plan in several ways. One of those ways is to determine how closely the company revenues have matched the annual projected budget during the years of the HOT Plan. Consistently, over a 14-year period that included a severe worldwide recession, Pitsco's actual income met or exceeded the projected annual budget, with actual revenues averaging 101 percent of the projected budget.

True Success

Students and Teachers Served

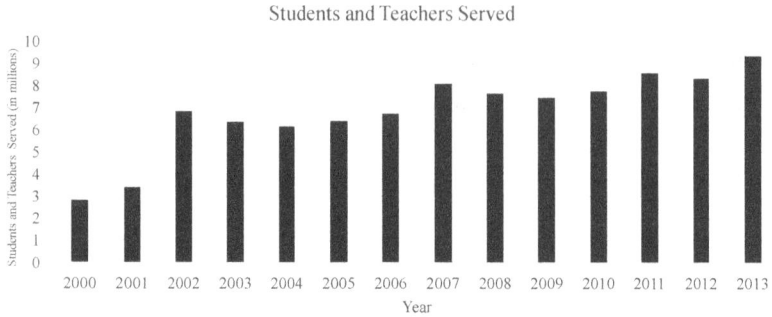

Chart 4: Number of Students and Teachers Served by Pitsco Products, 2000-2013

During those same years, students and teachers served by Pitsco educational solutions soared, climbing from 2.8 million to 9.3 million.

What Do Employees Say?

Global research studies on employee cultures affirm that highly engaged cultures outperform less engaged cultures, regardless of the country, economy, or social class.[39]

As seen on Pitsco's timeline, the numbers indicate increasing employee engagement, but do the employees themselves agree? And if they agree, how much do they attribute the highly engaged culture to the HOT Plan?

To dig into the answers to these questions, we designed two research studies in 2015, conducted in cooperation with a local university.

The studies were both qualitative (interview based) and quantitative (online survey based) and were conducted on the Pitsco main campus. Nearly 100 Pitsco employees participated in the two studies.

The question we explored in both studies was the same: Do changes in organizational structure also change organizational culture? And for our purposes, we asked its corollary: Have the HOT Plan's structural changes produced – indeed, even embedded – a highly engaged culture at Pitsco?

Using Giddens' theory[40] as a guideline, we first did a literature review of other studies about organizational culture around the world, getting our bearings on the interaction observed between structure and culture in other places. We later drew from the observations of these studies to interpret the results at Pitsco.

For this study, all interviews and surveys were conducted from a cross-section of employees and were unscripted. Identities of participants were kept anonymous.

The Qualitative Study

The first study, a qualitative study, was based on direct interviews. A diverse group of 10 Pitsco workers were invited to participate in the qualitative study.

Participants were not given a copy of the questions in advance, so all answers were extemporaneous. All interviews were individual and no individual overheard the answers of other members of the group.

Though the group was diverse in age, gender, and years of employment, their responses were remarkably similar.

The group was diverse in age, gender, and years of employment at Pitsco – both male and female, management as well as non-management, ranging from 18 months to more than 24 years of tenure, ranging in age from 30 to 62 years old. In spite of this diversity, their spontaneous responses overlapped and were remarkably similar.

For example, when asked to define a highly engaged employee in their own words, more than half of these participants identified a highly engaged employee as one who puts the good of the company ahead of his or her personal career goals. Six out of 10 responded that "having clear objectives and expectations" is a top factor in creating high employee engagement, along with "significance of work," "appreciation by supervisors," and a "sense of security."

Nine out of 10 interviewees rated Pitsco as above average in employee engagement. Their comments included praise for the listening skills of supervisors as well as praise for supervisor follow-up to those conversations. They also mentioned corporate transparency and communication as key elements to Pitsco's engaged culture.

All 10 employees identified the HOT Plan and the bonus check as a positive influence upon employee engagement at Pitsco. However, some employees responded that when work tasks fall outside of HOTs, employees are not as highly engaged. Also, some saw HOTs as both negative and positive.

"I can tell you from experience that the HOT Plan is one of the keys to employee engagement at Pitsco," said RB, a 61-year-old male who has worked at Pitsco for more than 10 years. "Everybody goes with the HOT Plan kicking and screaming every step of the way. We're all busy and then here come HOT Goals [HOTs]. But somehow, some way, they help us see the big picture. I think that's the key; you are forced to stop and think about the entirety of what you are doing."[41]

The Quantitative Study

To further test the culture of Pitsco from a wider base, we decided to run a carefully vetted online survey through the company email. The survey was based on the Organizational Culture Survey, created by sociologists Glaser, Zamanou, and Hacker (1987), but was modified slightly to personalize it to the Pitsco campus and available technology.[42]

Methodology for the Quantitative Study

Where the Survey Took Place

Research was conducted on the main campus of Pitsco, Inc. in Pittsburg, Kansas. Although Pitsco has another campus in Pittsburg and employees in the field around the United States, we chose employees located on the main campus. We did this in order to limit the number of variables that could be affecting the employees' view of culture. Our intent was to measure the effects of the HOT Plan.

> *Nine out of 10 interviewees rated Pitsco as above average in employee engagement.*

Participants and Procedures

The survey was conducted under the guidance of Pitsco employees Nancy, director of educator insights, and Stephanie, research coordinator. Nancy suggested that the survey be sent out through company email to make it simple for employees to respond. Surveys were emailed to the 152 employees located on the main campus over a three-day period; the survey was resent each day with an updated invitation to participate. During the three-day period, 87 opt-in responses were recorded and 82 surveys completed, representing more than half of the on-campus employees responding.

Demographics

Of the 82 participants who completed valid surveys, 33 identified as male and 49 identified as female. Participants also were asked to identify with one of five categories of tenure (years of employment) as Pitsco employees. The greatest number of participants, 47.6 percent (39 employees) had five years or less tenure, with the next two largest groups being 23.2 percent (19 employees) in the group of employees with six to 10 years of tenure and 17.1 percent (14 employees) of the employees with 21 years or more tenure at Pitsco. Employees from tenure groups of 11-15 years and 16-20 years had the least participation, with only 7.3 percent (six employees) and 4.9 percent (four employees), respectively. Since the HOT Plan is in its 17th year of practice at Pitsco, it is interesting to note that only employees in the top two tenure groups have experienced the culture of the company without the HOT Plan.

The Survey Instrument

The Organizational Culture Survey is made up of 36 questions divided into six subscales: Teamwork, Morale, Information Flow, Involvement, Supervision, and Meetings. We stayed true to the original version, with the following changes to the survey instrument:

- Generic references such as "this organization" were changed to say "Pitsco, Inc."
- Answers on the Organizational Culture Survey all are answered in a multiple-choice format using a Likert-type scale. We changed the language of responses from "extent" to "agree."
- The 36 questions were presented in a format that grouped them under their six subsets. This presentation was designed to minimize test fatigue by avoiding a long list of questions.
- Nancy also added a comment box for individual input at the end of the survey instrument to further validate the survey in the employees' minds.

The entire survey was taken online and scored via Survey Monkey. It was later analyzed through the IBM SPSS data-analysis program, courtesy of Pittsburg State University.

Results: The Significance of Sameness

The 36 statements about culture identified in the Organizational Culture Survey were phrased positively. They included statements such as "People I work with are direct and honest with each other," "Working here feels like being part of a family," and "I have a say in decisions that affect my work." Participants were asked to evaluate these positive cultural indicators based on how the following statements apply to them.

Since statements were worded positively, variance was revealed when employees or members of the organization disagreed. Sameness was created when participants agreed.

In response after response on the Pitsco campus, the answers to the survey revealed an astounding *sameness*. Across the board – regardless of the years of tenure with the company or the gender of the respondent – employee answers to all survey questions fell into the top two categories of "Agree" or "Strongly Agree." In fact, the statement "My supervisor gives criticism in a positive manner" received *100 percent* agreement by respondents.

High-engagement culture must be embedded.

Pause and consider the significance of this. How likely is it in any businesses of 200 or more employees that when the staff participated in an anonymous survey online, they would agree – 100 percent of them – that *all* of the company's supervisors give criticism in a positive manner? When we are looking to verify a deeply embedded, positive culture, this sameness speaks loudly. This unanimous response is clear evidence of a deeply embedded positive culture. Further results in the survey continued to reveal extremely high levels of agreement – an affirmation of the culture far above average.

But where does this leave us statistically? Most statistical analysis finds its nuggets of truth by digging into the statistical variance between answers. What is the significance of answers when little variance exists? What is the significance of sameness?

First, the virtual lack of any disagreement with the positive cultural statements on the Organizational Culture Survey indicates the obvious – that employees across all departments and levels of tenure and hierarchy are experiencing a consistent, positive culture. The only answer on the survey that showed any statistical variation pertained to how well supervisors *can take* criticism. On this one question, male employees were more in agreement than female employees that supervisors at Pitsco can take criticism well. With this exception, responses were homogenous.

In fact, out of the 36 statements, only nine statements fell below the 80-percent line of positive agreement. Five of those nine statements were in the final subscale of the test, the subscale called "Meetings." Although there is validity to this dip in agreement, test fatigue must be considered a possible influence when scores dip in the final section of a 36-question survey instrument.

It also must be noted that the week prior to this survey, a contract partner of Pitsco that employed a number of people on our main campus unexpectedly announced that it would be moving its base of operations, resulting in job loss. This unanticipated decision – a decision entirely outside of Pitsco's control – no doubt influenced some of the lower scores noted on subscales dealing with job security, including "Understand reasons changes are made" and "Know what's happening in other work areas," which fell to 69 and 52 percent agreement, respectively.

Relating to Other Research

Using Sirisetti's idea of employee engagement, we found that Pitsco culture scores indicated support for the hypothesis that the HOT Plan shaped the highly engaged culture of Pitsco.[43]

Sirisetti's markers of an embedded, high-engagement culture include a sense of employee empowerment, job motivation, and organizational commitment and trust. These areas correlate with the Organizational Culture Survey in high involvement (Subsets 2 and 4), employee empowerment (Subsets 2 and 5), job motivation (Subsets 2 and 3), and organizational commitment and trust (Subsets 1, 2, 4, and 5). Pitsco scored "Agree" or "Strongly Agree" in all of these categories when ranked independently by employees.

Further, employees gave high agreement to all questions related to teamwork. This indicates a strong sense of group and team identity – a factor directly related to the team-based HOT Plan. This team-based structure guards Pitsco against the toxic "me-centricity" attitude, identified by Irwin as the death of high engagement.[44]

Limitations of the Study

The statistical indication that females may be experiencing supervision differently and more negatively than males bears further investigation. More research should be done in this area. The productiveness of meetings also was indicated as a weaker area, with "Agree" and "Strongly Agree" responses to positive meeting experiences falling to only 58-65 percent. Holding effective business meetings, however, is an area of continuous improvement for most organizations and Pitsco is no exception.

Future research for the HOT Plan cultural impact at Pitsco should consider dividing the tenured employees into two groups – those who were employed by Pitsco prior to the HOT Plan and those who were employed by Pitsco after the HOT Plan began.

Finally, Pitsco practices a strong appreciation of its employees that extends beyond the boundaries of the HOT Plan. It is important for other companies considering the HOT Plan to note that our deeply embedded sense of community and collegiality could be due to these other appreciation efforts as well. The celebration of employee birthdays, years of service, and above-and-beyond work performance given at monthly company-wide luncheons are a few examples of Pitsco's ongoing culture of appreciation and recognition of employees.

Conclusions

The characteristics of enthusiasm, loyalty, job satisfaction, longevity of job tenure, and a willingness to go above-and-beyond what is required – all markers of highly engaged employees – were present in 100 percent of the respondents in the interview-based qualitative study. The survey-based quantitative study also reflected highly engaged attitudes through the dominance of "Agree" and "Strongly Agree" responses to all survey questions. In addition, the responses to all 36 questions were in the "Agree" and "Strongly Agree" categories more than 50 percent of the time, with the lowest score on any question sitting at 52 percent "Agree" and "Strongly Agree" and the highest score hitting unanimity, with 100 percent of participants choosing "Agree" and "Strongly Agree" responses on one question.

Qualities and attitudes like these – across age groups and years of service (tenure) among Pitsco employees – tell us that the HOT Plan is working and that it is more than an incentive plan. It is a game changer.

Our hypothesis – that the HOT Plan has shaped a positive, highly engaged workplace – is fully supported by these studies, both in quantitative and in qualitative research. The steadily increasing number of students and teachers served and the company's consistency in exceeding the projected budget confirms the bottom line advantage as well.

So now the choice is yours. The numbers have spoken. Two decades of Pitsco archives and two research studies done on the Pitsco culture have proven that the HOT Plan works for us.

Will you let it work for you?

Chapter 13 Postscript: The Charted Data

Pitsco Culture Quantitative Study – Specific Numbers and Charts

For those who like to read the numbers and view the charts, we include the following summaries. Information is organized by subscale; N represents the number of respondents that completed each question. This information only indicates the percentage of answers that fell into the "Agree" or "Strongly Agree" scale.

Pitsco Quantitative Research Survey – Subscales

Chart 1: Teamwork

Coworkers:	N	% Agree	% Strongly Agree	Total %
Are direct and honest	73	60.3	37.0	97.3
Accept criticism	74	51.4	23.0	74.4
Resolve disagreements	74	58.1	32.4	90.5
Function as a team	73	43.8	49.3	93.1
Are cooperative and considerate	74	43.2	54.1	97.3
Confront problems constructively	74	51.4	35.1	86.5
Are good listeners	74	59.5	32.4	91.9
Are caring	74	41.9	56.8	98.7

Teamwork

■ % Agree · % Strongly Agree

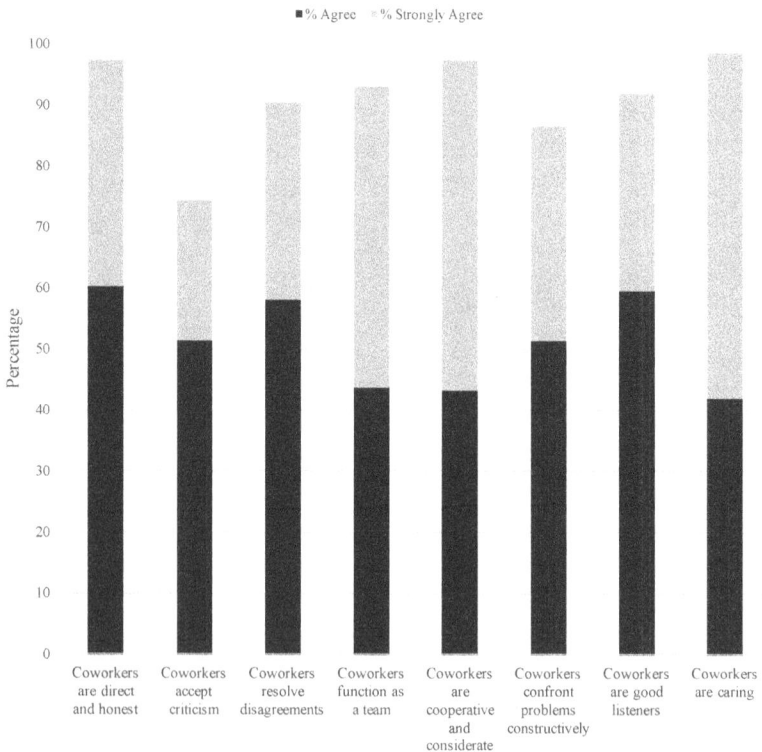

Chart 2: Morale

	N	% Agree	% Strongly Agree	Total %
Employee/Management have productive working relationship	71	54.9	29.6	84.5
Pitsco motivates to put out best efforts	72	45.8	47.2	93.0
Respects its workers	72	44.4	50.0	94.4
Treats people in a consistently fair manner	73	50.7	34.2	84.9
Feels like being part of a family	72	33.3	52.8	86.1
Atmosphere of trust	72	45.8	37.5	83.3
Motivates people to be efficient and productive	72	47.2	44.4	91.6

Morale

■ % Agree □ % Strongly Agree

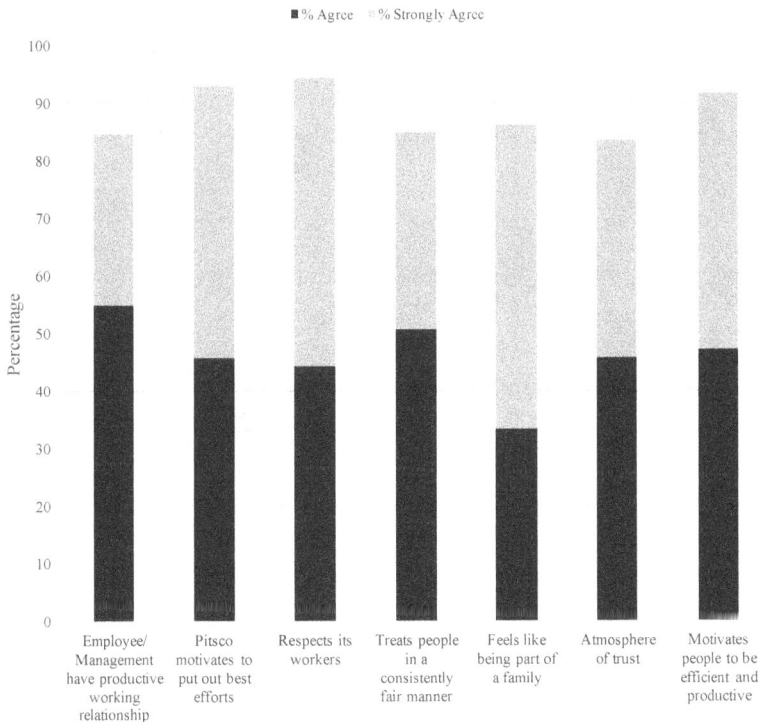

Chart 3: Information Flow

	N	% Agree	% Strongly Agree	Total %
Understand big picture	71	50.7	35.2	85.9
Understand reasons changes are made	71	38.0	31.0	69.0
Know what's happening in other work areas	71	38.0	14.1	52.1
Get information needed to do job well	71	59.2	25.4	84.6

Information Flow

■ % Agree   ▦ % Strongly Agree

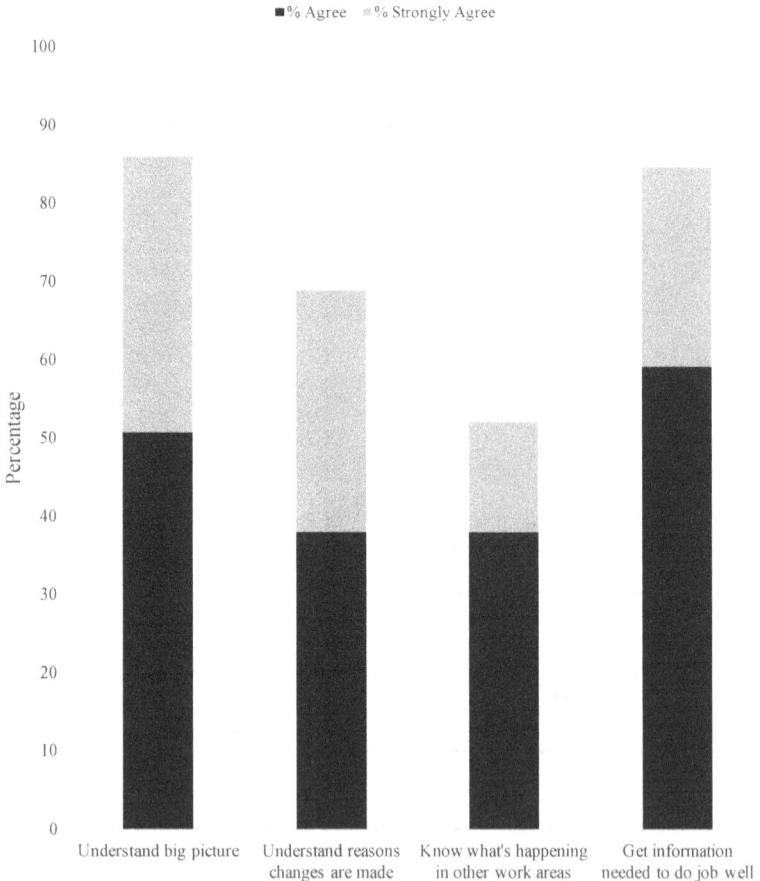

Chart 4: Involvement

	N	% Agree	% Strongly Agree	Total %
Have a say in decisions that affect my work	71	56.3	22.5	78.8
Asked to make suggestions about how to do job better	71	56.3	31.0	87.3
Pitsco values ideas of workers at every level	70	40.0	37.1	77.1
My opinions count at Pitsco	71	50.7	22.5	73.2

Involvement

■ % Agree　▫ % Strongly Agree

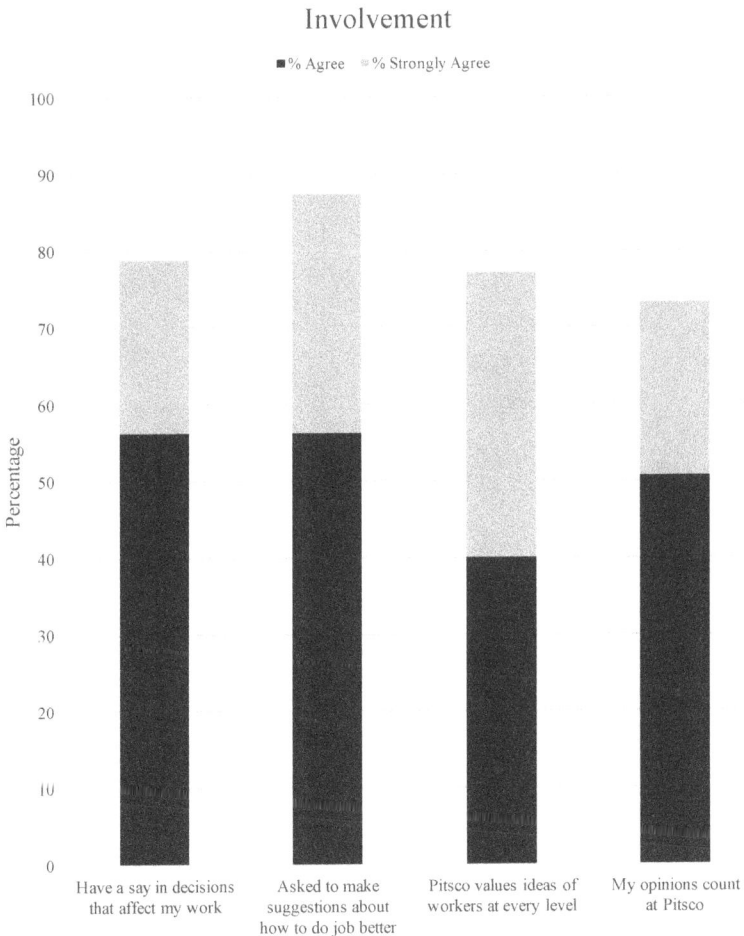

Chart 5: Supervision

Supervisor:	N	% Agree	% Strongly Agree	Total %
Makes job requirements clear	68	60.3	35.3	95.6
Acknowledges good job	69	46.4	47.8	94.2
Takes criticism well	68	50.0	27.9	77.9
Delegates responsibility	69	50.7	44.9	95.6
Is approachable	68	33.8	63.2	97.0
Gives criticism in a positive manner	69	50.0	50.0	100
Is a good listener	69	40.6	50.7	91.3
Tells me how I'm doing	69	44.9	44.9	89.8

Supervision

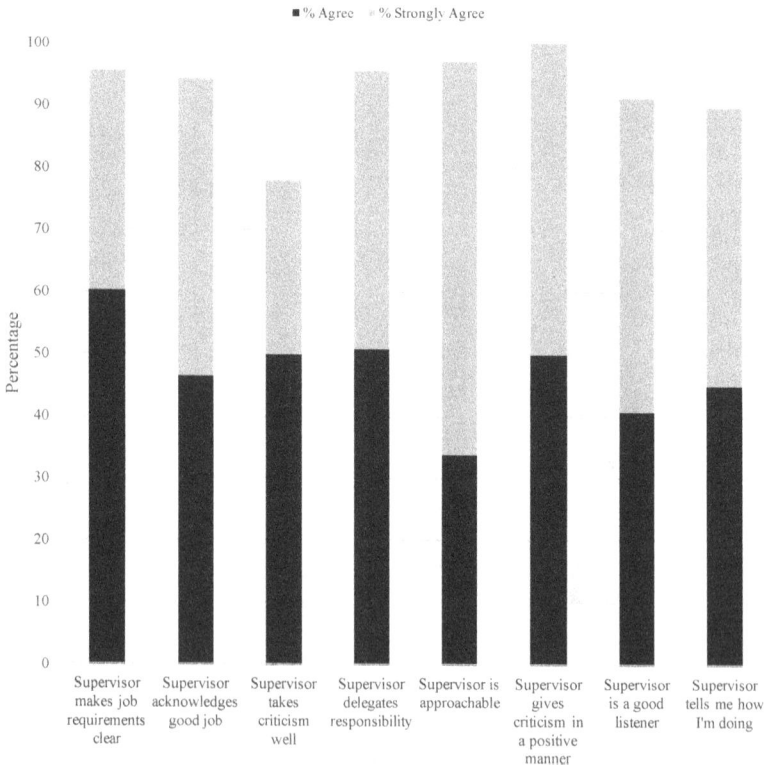

Chart 6: Meetings

	N	% Agree	% Strongly Agree	Total %
Decisions get put into action	67	56.7	19.4	76.1
Everyone takes part in discussions	69	47.8	17.4	65.2
Discussions stay on track	67	44.8	17.9	62.7
Time is well spent	68	39.7	19.1	58.8
Tap creative potential of people present	68	39.7	19.1	58.8

Meetings

■ % Agree ░ % Strongly Agree

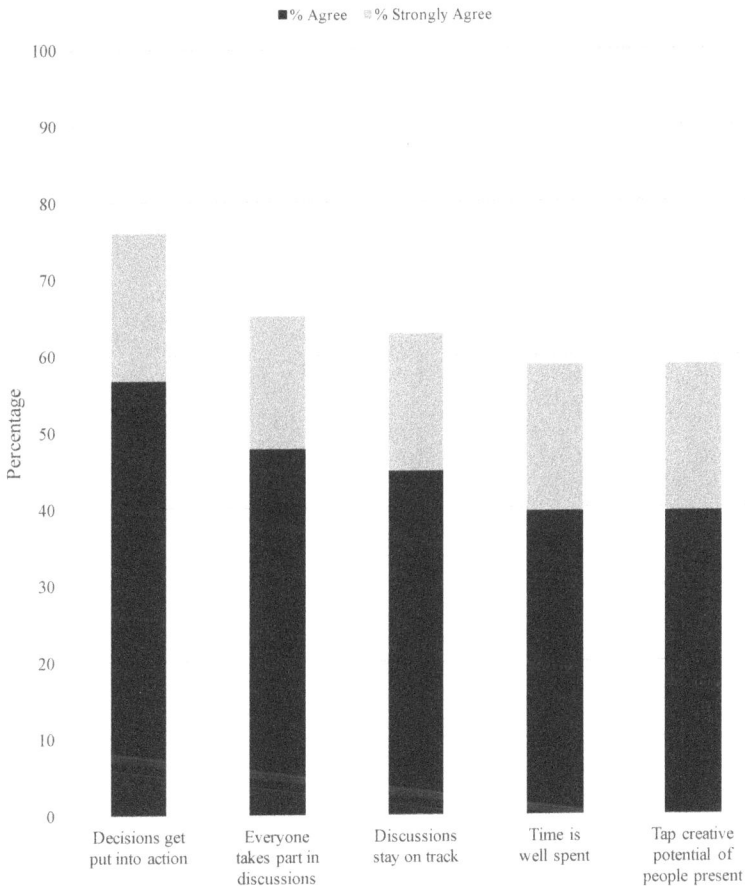

Chapter Fourteen

HOT Vision

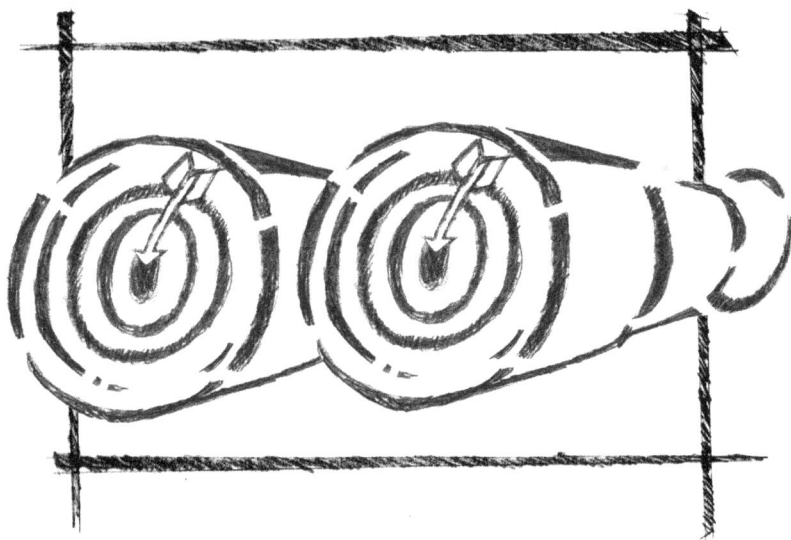

Enduring vision is something that is built over time.

Some might argue that a vision statement is the first step in setting up a new company, but in reality, this is not true for most enterprises. Instead, most businesses are launched by a Big Idea. The Big Idea – whether an innovative product, a better service, or a new way to solve an old problem – is what the entrepreneur believes he or she has to offer the world. But while the Big Idea has the energy to launch a business, it does not have the enduring strength of a vision to sustain a business over the long haul. The original idea might generate excitement, but it is likely to be too broad, too fuzzy, and too tenuous to provide the firm and enduring foundation your business requires.

Pitsco launched as a company without a written vision statement, although in my gut, I understood our vision from the beginning, even if I hadn't put the right words to it. Perhaps the phrase "Fast, friendly service" printed on our first ad sheets foretold some of the essentials that would ultimately help us succeed. "Fast, friendly service" eventually became a pillar of our brand.

But the truth is, our company existed for 20 years before we arrived at the written vision statement we have now. A company obviously can go a very long time – and even achieve a level of success – without a clarified definition of its vision.

However, clarifying vision is eventually necessary if your business is to endure, so you should strive to crystallize your vision statement when you feel you have a good grasp on it. Even though I understood our vision in my gut, it wasn't enough just for me, as the founder of the company, to understand the vision or even for a select handful of people at the top of the organization to share it. A clear understanding of vision is critical for all your employees in order to implement the HOT Plan effectively.

Sometimes, there is confusion about the difference between a vision statement and a mission statement. Stated simply, a vision statement answers the "Why" of your business, and a mission statement answers the "How" of your production and service. Two fundamental questions that help to clarify both the vision and the mission for any business endeavor are "Why are we doing this?" and "How do we do it well?"

Leadership has a duty to clarify the company vision.

In our years before the HOT Plan, Pitsco crafted a mission statement – a statement that identified how we would go about achieving our goals – and the statement served its purpose. But since the HOT Plan began, we haven't needed a mission statement. The HOT Plan provides the way to answer the how question through the HOT Targets that map out the process by which our work will get done.

However, the why question remained. The deeper why questions – why you get up and go to work each morning, why you do this type of work in the first place, and ultimately, why your organization even exists – also must be answered in the vision statement. At a certain point for the leadership of our company, it became necessary to clarify and establish our company vision and to capture it in an effective and brief statement.

"Why" It Matters

Even though the question of why begs for an answer every single day – every morning when we go to work and every evening when we head back home – some organizations never even get around to asking, "Why?" The only question in the forefront of their business mind is, "What's next?"

But human beings are made for purpose. No matter how long a business puts it off, the question of why will stand waiting in the wings until it is answered. Many leaders fill their business calendars with activities to keep themselves too busy for the serious consideration of purpose. But meaningful, enduring success is reserved for those leaders and organizations that take time to figure out their why and clearly grasp their vision – their *raison d'être*.

Companies Change

The need to know your why becomes greater as your company changes and grows. All healthy companies change – they increase in complexity as they grow. As complexity increases, there is always the risk that an organization that was once clearly focused on its vision will find its sense of purpose diluted or its focus distracted. As the employee ranks of Pitsco began to swell, we found ourselves swept up in distracting forces before we knew it – dabbling in more and more different things. It didn't take long for us to feel a strong need to clarify exactly what we were about and return to our basics. A good vision statement is a tool that helps a maturing company navigate the stages of its own progress.

A good vision statement is a tool that helps a company navigate the stages of its own progress.

Generations Change

Each new generation brings its own peculiarities and strengths to the marketplace. Today's generation of young workers – the millennials – is the single most why-oriented generation that we've ever had in America. Sociologists sometimes call this group Generation Y, but I have another name for them: "Generation Why?"

I marvel at the millennials. They have more options available to them in terms of education and vocation than most generations but are more hesitant to commit themselves to a company for the long haul. Their focus is on the why of the work: Why is this work important in the larger world? What cause can the company support through its profits? Even in times of recession when jobs were scarce, millennials still asked why before taking jobs. Good pay and benefits were not the only answers they expected to hear.

> *If you can't explain the why to millennials, they won't have much interest in sticking with you.*

As the millennial generation moves into the position of being the majority of the worldwide workforce, vision is becoming more important than ever. If a company has a meaningful vision and pursues that vision with honesty and integrity, that company will find millennials signing on with it. By the same token, if you can't explain to millennials why they are doing something, they won't have much interest in sticking with it.

However, why-centric thinking is a good thing for organizations with HOT Plans. The reason is simple: Everyone in a HOT Plan organization has the potential to be a leader and participates by creating targets that shape the future of the company. Creating good targets requires understanding the big questions that the company faces. A generation well practiced in asking why has what it takes to make great HOT Plan leaders.

In the long run, this is a very good trait to have in your employees, particularly if you need employees that are creative self-starters. And if you have read this far and are still interested in the HOT Plan, my guess is that you probably do.

Creating a Vision Statement

Don't let all this talk of the weighty significance of the vision statement make you sweat. Creating the vision statement at Pitsco was actually a fun process, and it should be for you as well. The process gives a chance to bounce ideas around and share perspectives and get to know the people in your company a little better. As you share ideas, you will discover more about how your people view the company and its existing legacy and what their hopes and dreams are for your company's future.

We took a collaborative approach to the creation of the vision statement. We didn't involve all our employees, but we did bring all the members of our management team – heads of the various company divisions – into the process. In the creation of a vision statement, this level of collaboration is normal; it yields a broader employee buy-in than if the CEO or top leadership writes the statement.

Even though the CEO – perhaps even the founder of your organization – has a very powerful vision in mind, it is important that the expression of the vision isn't myopic. If your desire is to grant responsibility to all employees, people throughout your organization must recognize in your vision statement the aspects about your company that they cherish. The best way to ensure that this happens is to build the statement cooperatively with employees of multiple viewpoints. This ensures that you build a vision that benefits from the collective wisdom of all those participating in the process. It also ensures that there is room for everyone at the table of influence in your company.

Our vision statement has remained a solid guide for Pitsco for 20 years, a testament to the fact that it is worth the investment of time and resources to get your vision statement right.

When we created our vision statement, we brought in an advisor to guide us through the process, a gentleman from Alabama named Stephan. It was clear to everyone right away that he had a mind for Big

Ideas and a way with words that was all his own. He also had a knack for cutting right to the heart of things.

The first time Stephan visited Pitsco he took a quick look at our records and asked, "Is Pitsco an education company or a furniture company?"

I was a little shocked at the question, but I replied that we were an education company. Stephan looked quizzical and pointed out that Pitsco's invoices indicated that most of the money we pulled in at the time was from sales of desks for schools, a product we had only ever intended as a peripheral support for our main line of curriculum. The point was clear. We had a schism in our identity, and we had some work to do in clarifying exactly why we were in business.

Actually, we liked Stephan so much that we ended up hiring him, and Pitsco works closely with him to this day. The process he guided us through was one he had used with other companies. It worked so well for us that I'd like to relate it to you.

Step by Step

First, we brought all of our most prominent company leaders together. This meant all of our division leaders. For another organization without formal divisions, this simply would mean bringing in proven leaders – perhaps department heads – the ones with the knowledge and commitment to represent all the various parts of the organization.

With everyone together, we began a discussion about the shared values and principles of the group. We wanted to make sure we had something approaching a common vision among us, even if we didn't quite have the words nailed down to express it. Stephan inspired the group with a talk about the expansiveness of a strong vision and the important role it plays in the company's identity and future.

A Process for Creating a Vision Statement

1	Bring company leaders together.
2	Have each person write a sentence describing the company vision. Share the sentences with the group.
3	Have each person choose one noun, verb, and adjective/adverb from their sentence – three words only. On a board, create a short list of these words.
4	Discuss them as a group and pare the list down further to two or three words in each category.
5	Create a new, single sentence using only these words – no new nouns, verbs, adjectives, or adverbs.

"Now you're going to need your pen and paper," he told us after we were all stirred up. "Everyone, write down one sentence describing your vision for the future."

Everyone had their thinking caps on at this point. We were thinking big, and for several of us in the room, the sentence grew and grew until it was as long as a paragraph – or even longer. We privately honed and perfected them. We wanted to get all of our thoughts written into one eloquent and impressive string of words. When everyone was done and basically happy with what they had written, Stephan directed us to read them aloud.

There were some doozies – some really brilliant thinking going on in the room that day. We were all smiling; everyone seemed pretty satisfied with their work. Next came the painful part.

"Now, everybody choose one noun, one verb, and one adjective or adverb from your sentence," Stephan said. "And no more."

The faces around the room showed that there was some angst about this. How could we preserve the meaning of an elaborate thought in just three words? Well, we couldn't. What we could do instead was quickly discover the most essential part of that thought, the part of the statement that we couldn't live without. This was a tough assignment. Soon enough, though, the job was done.

Noun	Verb	Adjective/Adverb
Product	Create	Cool
Students	Lead	Educational
Success	Change	

After this assignment, the three-word groups all went up on the board, organized by noun, verb, and adjective/adverb. Then, the process of discussion and paring down of the words began. We looked at each of the words listed individually as well as grouped with the other words on the board list. If one word had been repeated multiple times, we made note of it. That signaled to us that the word probably approached something essential. If words were similar but not quite the same in meaning, we discussed those differences. Was one of them closer to what we wanted? Was one of them more encompassing? Was there a way to represent both concepts in a single word, or was one of the concepts simply not hitting the mark? If there was a word on the board that seemed to stick out like a sore thumb, it probably was an outlier. We didn't want to exclude the thing that was most important to anyone, but we also were looking to find our common vision. It was a delicate balance.

Now we were getting somewhere. This felt exciting. I could recognize my company in this cluster of words, but the words also told me how the others I had hired and worked with every day envisioned it.

Next, Stephan directed everyone to use the words on the short list to create a single sentence from them, using only connecting prepositions and articles – no new nouns, verbs, adjectives, or adverbs. We weren't obliged to use every word, but we were encouraged to try to capture the spirit of the whole. After we each read our sentences, Stephan asked us to vote on which sentence we liked best and refine a vision statement from that one.

We ended up adding the word *positively* during that refining discussion and came up with the statement: "To lead educational change that positively affects students." A little later down the road, we changed the word *students* to *learners* because we realized the scope of our vision went beyond schools. Many years later, we shortened it again to the vision statement we use today: *leading education that positively affects learners.*

Hallmarks of a Strong Vision Statement	
Clarity	easily understood
Concise	one sentence
Specific	concrete information
Broad	an umbrella statement that keeps your business on track in times of change

This process certainly isn't the only process for creating a vision statement, but it worked well for us. The statement our company produced had several essential qualities. The statement was clear – a hallmark of a good vision statement. Nobody had to scratch their head and puzzle out business jargon to figure out what it means. The statement is concise. As Thomas Jefferson once said, "The most valuable of all talents [is] that of never using two words where one will do."[45] A vision statement is made more powerful when it is contained in as few words as possible. It is specific. It tells who we serve, in what domain we serve them, and how we serve them. At the same time, it is broad. This is not a contradiction. Even though it is specific, the language allows the vision statement to maintain focus even if and when situations change.

Communicate Your Vision

Once we had the statement clearly in hand, we made a point of using the new vision statement at every opportunity. We recited it in every meeting and emblazoned it on cards, paper, and signs above doors – posted wherever employees might see it. To this day, I still call on the group to shout out our vision at employee get-togethers. The vision statement has lasted us about 20 years now and has remained relevant the entire time. If you stop any one of Pitsco's employees and ask them what the vision statement is, they'll almost certainly be able to tell you. Because we rehearse it so often, the staff all know we respect it and they know that we expect them to respect it as well.

Ask our employees today what our vision statement is – they'll almost certainly be able to tell you.

The vision statement is the starting point for your HOT Plan's success and the center point of your organization's culture. Treat it with respect once you have unleashed it into your company. This means talking about it, owning it, and making it the reference point for business decisions day in and day out. A great vision statement brings along benefits, but it also makes demands on you and your organization. Like any empowering ideal, it can chafe at times to live up to the statement. Remember this: the vision statement represents the company's high road, but the high road isn't always the easiest route.

Sometimes a company changes its vision statement. I want to give a word of caution here. Changing your vision statement is a tricky business and in all honesty, I believe you do this at your own peril. When you tamper with a vision statement, you are tampering not only with the very reason people came to work at your company but also with the existing culture of your organization. Fine-tuning is one thing (our change from *students* to *learners*, for example), but a company's culture will reel if broad reconsiderations of the "Why?" are entertained.

> *The vision statement represents the company's high road, but the high road isn't always the easiest route.*

For example, Pitsco has many of the core competencies of a movie production company, and in our education work, we do extensive audio/video production. We write scripts, make storyboards, and deal with talent agencies and outside writers. Pitsco's skill base has a lot of overlap with a film production company, but it would be far-fetched to imagine that we would change our vision statement to something such as "To lead cinematic change that positively affects audiences." That would never work for us. We have attracted Pitsco employees who cherish education and the opportunity to lead educational change that positively affects learners.

Drastically changing a company vision is rare and usually only is done as a desperate move for survival – when a company finds that they must make swift changes or perish. But there are other, more subtle ways to abandon a company vision. Most often a vision is abandoned when a company simply fails to live up to it. If the vision is allowed to languish, the ideals of your organization and the culture you have built upon them will languish as well.

Enduring Vision

Companies that survive the rocky start-up phase and achieve stability later might find themselves to be victims of their own success. Competition and market changes can later threaten their stability. A company must be able to adapt without losing its core identity and culture. For this reason, a vision statement must be broad and enduring.

All companies go through life stages. Anyone who has had a few courses in organizational theory will recognize a pattern that repeats itself in the life of any business that survives its start-up phase. The pattern itself is pretty simple.

A company must be able to adapt without losing its core identity and culture.

Phase A in any business is entrepreneurial. The focus is on start-up issues, growing volume, creating change, and dealing with change. It can be a bumpy yet exciting time to be involved in any organization.

A company enters Phase B when a clear direction can be seen in the market and the company has begun to take shape as a business. Now, the emphasis shifts to firming up that shape and cementing the company's aims and culture. New goals are set. The adolescent organization is not out of the danger zone yet, however. Order has been glimpsed, but it still is developing. Leadership is creating the processes that will sustain and govern the organization. Structure becomes more important and the need for a clear vision is felt more keenly.

Companies that successfully navigate Phase B will hit Phase C – they will begin to reach their potential within the present circumstances. Things level out and everyone takes a breather.

But just as things calm down and level out, it seems the market does all within its power to introduce disruption into the life of a company. It is said that nature abhors a vacuum, and in like manner, it seems that the business world abhors a status quo. New competitors arise to get in on the success, innovations challenge the supremacy of the company's product, and new paradigms rise up to challenge the company's relevance. There may be some low-innovation industries that seem to escape this – such as paper goods or the tire industry – but this is not the norm. Even within low-innovation industries, the timeline of disruption is only slowed, not halted. This is why, when your business hits a period of market change, your vision must be broad and enduring.

Your vision statement is the centerpiece of your culture.

An example of a product that experienced disruption and had to adapt is rayon – the first synthetic fiber, manufactured from wood pulp. Rayon's first important application was as a filament in tires, with its critical use in tires during World War II. Later, the tire industry began to use steel-belted tires instead of rayon. When the original primary demand for rayon went away, the industry faced a crisis. Several enterprising engineers were called together to study new uses for the fiber, and today, rayon is a versatile fabric used in many industries. It is used not only in the apparel industry but also as the primary fiber in many common hygienic and medical products, including diapers, surgical gauze, and dialysis machines. If the manufacturer's vision had been limited to tires or the war effort, this transition might not have occurred.[46]

The education industry has also seen sweeping transformative changes in recent years. In the '90s, we faced the rise of digital media and computer technology, starting a cascade of transitions in communication that have shaken the very foundations of how and where we learn. From the current push for STEM education to the increasing demand for 24/7 beyond-the-schoolhouse learning, educational change requires Pitsco to keep a keen focus on its vision. The vision statement we hammered out so many years ago keeps us from being tossed about by these changes, anchoring our purpose and enabling us to navigate our way through them.

Your organization will face disruptive issues if it hasn't already. This is universal to all organizations – not only businesses but also nonprofits, religious organizations, teams, and schools. When your organization experiences a cycle of disruption, you will probably have to make some changes in what you do and how you do it. But with a good vision statement, you won't have to change your why. A solid vision statement helps you navigate your way through the transition without losing your way – and your identity – in the process.

Chapter Fifteen

HOT Success

W ho is carrying the locus of responsibility for your success? This is a critical question, because according to the US Bureau of Labor Statistics, half of all business start-ups tend to fail within five years.[47] But if you have the right people carrying the locus of responsibility for accomplishing the vision of your organization, your business does not have to be one of them.

As we have said throughout this book, the secret of enduring success in your business begins with clarity of vision followed by clarity of communication and then takes a leap forward when the employees are empowered to accept the locus of responsibility for their work. Success is kept on track when you have a system to ensure that the organization's goals will move beyond hopes and dreams and instead become targets of accomplishment.

> *The values of the HOT Plan are timeless keys in sync with the basics of human nature.*

All of these elements are incorporated in the HOT Plan. The values of the HOT Plan – the power of ownership, personal responsibility, and accountability – are timeless keys to business transformation that are fundamentally in sync with the basic motivations of human nature.

The seed of the HOT Plan was planted through a boys' track team, so we know it works with sports teams. But what about other non-business settings? Does the HOT Plan work for them? I suggest that it does. In this chapter, I want to tell you three more stories designed to stretch your vision. As you read them, let your imagination take flight and imagine how the HOT Plan can bring success to many other areas in your life.

Winning the Right Race

When it came to being a track star, Charlie was the kind of kid who didn't need a medal to prove to himself he was capable of great success. Even if he'd never run an event before, he still was sure he could beat the state record if only given the opportunity.

At Charlie's first track meet, the official in charge of his event gathered the pack of runners and asked if any of them could run a four-minute mile. At that time, the four-minute-mile high school track record was the big news in high school athletics and belonged to one runner: Jim Ryun, now a Kansas University distance runner. In 1964, Ryun was the first high school athlete to run the mile in less than four minutes; he went on to win a silver medal in the 1968 Olympic Games.

Charlie didn't need a medal to prove to himself he was capable of great success.

But that day, when the official asked the small group of Oklahoma student-athletes reporting for the mile run if there were any four-minute-mile runners, Charlie's hand shot up.

"That's me!" he said and jumped to his feet. In truth, Charlie had never even run the mile race before.

"You can run a four-minute mile?" the official asked.

"Yes, sir," he replied.

"Alright then," the official said after sizing up Charlie's slight stature. "You're checked in."

Charlie was a little guy with limited successes in life. He was a simple kid and had challenges with anything that required hard-core academic skills.

But Charlie had two things going for him: he would follow directions and he possessed unstoppable enthusiasm.

Charlie shot off the starter line on that hot, dusty Oklahoma afternoon and quickly sped to the lead. He led the pack on the first lap of the four-lap race at an astonishing pace. He sped past the starting line and kept his stride for lap two. By the end of lap two, his lead was dropping, but he still had the race easily in hand. He pushed with all he had as the third lap began.

Frankly, I had never seen him run like this in practice. Like any good coach, I taught my runners to save some strength for the last lap, not give it all away in the first three. I was on my feet with the rest of the team, cheering Charlie on – but admittedly, I was concerned.

Then he hit the wall. By the end of lap three, Charlie's energy level shut down. He lost the lead and fell back as the other runners passed him by. In fact, he not only came in last, he could barely jog across the finish line. One thing all of my athletes knew was that they had to finish their race. If they finished, their coach would be proud of them.

I ran down on the field and walked with Charlie as he cooled down.

"I'm so sorry, Mr. Dean," he said. "I tried my best. Next track meet, can I run the 660?"

"Well no, Charlie," I said. "That race is only for junior high runners."

"But Mr. Dean," he said, "I'm only in ninth grade."

Ninth grade was the highest level of junior high. Then it hit me. I had entered Charlie in the wrong level and thus, the wrong event. He shouldn't be competing in the mile race until his 10th-grade year. The following meet I correctly entered him in the 660 and he ran well.

Charlie became determined to bring home medals as he followed the instructions on his 3" x 5" cards at every track practice. The cards, which spelled out his daily targets, put the locus of responsibility in Charlie's hands to prepare for his track event. He was single-minded and consistent. He showed up every day, got his card, and completed every exercise. Charlie began coming home with medals.

I left Weleetka High School the year before Charlie was a senior, but his success in track continued and he reached the state level that year. He won the mile run event and the team was a top finisher at the state track meet that year. Charlie was among the best of them.

Charlie wasn't a champion in football, basketball, or academics; but he was a champion in track. It was the HOT Plan that prepared him to become a track champion. The individualized workout cards gave Charlie daily targets that prepared him to win his events. In today's HOT Plan language, the team's "Must Win Challenges" were winning district and regional meets and qualifying team members for state. One "Key Initiative" for the Weleetka team was to win the most points possible in as many events as possible. Charlie's personal HOT Target was to place in the mile race, his only event, evidenced by winning a track-meet medal and thus contributing points for the team.

Lessons in Education

Middle school students are gregarious little wonders. A blast to be around, kids of this age have a strong natural enthusiasm and a deep desire to make a good impression. They are easily excited about what they are learning; school is often still vibrant and enthralling to them. In the classroom, sixth graders see the teacher as the king or queen, a fountain of knowledge and a figure of authority. But something seems to happen right around seventh grade. The positive attitudes begin to change.

Seventh-grade students who once thought school was cool seem to change overnight. Now some of these same students think they are too cool for school, while others feel small and overwhelmed. What causes this? For one thing, the structure of school changes radically in seventh grade. A classroom and social situation that they once found fun and navigable now seems uncomfortable and hostile. Hormones, social pressures, and a radically different institutional environment cause many students to lose their grip on engagement with learning.

At this age, kids are expected to become more independent. But unfortunately, the feeling of empowerment that was carefully fostered by many elementary classroom teachers is sapped away in middle school by more adult teaching methods. For students, this change is often accompanied by a daunting loss of purpose. What relevance does what they are learning in school have to the rest of their lives? Combine this with social stigmas that limit their self-confidence – such as the widespread assumptions that kinesthetically oriented kids are not very smart or that girls are not good in math – and some seventh-grade students wonder why it is even worth trying.

Seventh-grade students seem to change overnight.

"What does it matter anyway? I can't do it and I'll never use this stuff in the real world anyway," they say.

Welcome to the middle school experience of many students. Too often, these are the ingredients in a recipe for the loss of student ownership and accountability in their education. Unfortunately, the trend deepens in eighth grade.

Pitsco wanted to find a way to step into this challenging situation. But we needed a methodology specifically for middle school learners. The result of our quest was the creation of a curriculum and a system: Synergistic Systems. As the program expanded, the name was changed to Pitsco Modules.

Pitsco Modules are a learning system. To change the middle school experience, we changed the learning environment as well as the curriculum. Modules are marketed as a classroom lab experience. The full package includes new furniture, new curricula, and new methods – even for the teacher. The newness of the environment and the method by which the content is experienced casts a spell on kids and sends a message that old assumptions about school do not apply here.

And they don't.

In a traditional sage on the stage classroom, the teacher carries the locus of responsibility for the content and learning that takes place. The subject matter typically is presented as a lecture for note-taking or lists to be memorized before the next test. Pitsco Modules move the locus of responsibility for the content to be learned from the teacher to the students. Students work in pairs and rotate through workstations that guide them through learning experiences. The entire curriculum is hands on. Abstract ideas become physically real to students through the synergistic learning process.

In addition, Modules continually refer to the subject matter's connection to the world of work and often take their titles from career fields, such as *Applied Physics*, *Hotel Management*, *Oceanography*, and *Research & Design*. Students are reminded again and again that what they are doing in a Modules lab has a future purpose. They are exploring the possibilities of their own careers and gaining skills relevant to those possibilities. This encourages them to take ownership of their work because if they do a good job, it isn't just about a grade, it is about gaining ownership over their future.

The single greatest tool for giving middle school kids a feeling of ownership is to put them in charge of directing their own learning. Each Module title has a series of audio/video presentations every learner must complete, but the teams work through the material independently from the teacher and the rest of the class. Pairs work at their own pace through the presentations and hands-on projects and not only teach themselves but learn from each other.

I remember visiting a Modules lab with a teacher I'd come to know. In one of our first labs, the space the school had granted for the lab was hardly ideal – under the gym bleachers in an area shared with a traditional shop class. Tools and supplies were kept in two offstage dressing rooms nearby. The teacher invited me to visit and observe his class, but I honestly wasn't yet sure what it was he wanted me to see. When I asked about this, the teacher was noncommittal.

"Just watch," he said. "Later we can talk about what you see."

Pretty soon a kid came in the lab. I quickly put together that this student had an intellectual disability, a fact later confirmed by the teacher. This was a learner who wasn't capable of keeping up in a traditional classroom and therefore experienced very little success in school.

He sat down at the *Electricity* Module next to his student partner, got out the materials for a wiring project, and got to work. First, they accessed a video and began watching the instructions for the project. At this point, his process of learning began to arrest my attention.

> *Give middle school kids ownership*
> *by putting them in charge*
> *of their own learning.*

He watched part of the video, stopped it, rewound it, and watched it again. Over and over, he watched it in bits, as if to take it in only one sip at a time. Simultaneously, he was working the required wiring project. Now, electricity isn't exactly easy subject matter and the project wasn't a simple, paint-by-numbers kind of thing. The project required real thinking on the part of the student. He repeated the process of replaying the video in short clips and then applying the information for 10 or 15 minutes until he finally got his project done. All the while, his student partner was very patient with him, methodically talking through the process with the boy, never rushing him.

So here the intellectually disabled boy was, quietly learning about electricity at his own pace in a Modules lab located under the bleachers of a gym, with another student as his teacher and friend.

And he was succeeding.

He was doing the same work as any other student, something that would not have been possible in a regular classroom. The intellectually disabled learner who had never known academic success before was now taking ownership of his own education. His non-disabled partner was not only learning the subject matter and completing the assignment himself but also learning valuable life lessons in patience, service to others, and accountability.

Suddenly the beauty of what was happening hit me.

Suddenly the beauty of what was happening hit me and it became an emotional moment. I had to fight back the tears. This boy was being offered a chance to succeed in life.

This same story happens a thousand times a day in classrooms across America by kids using Pitsco Modules. Learners who have been left behind by traditional methodology experience educational success when given the locus of responsibility for their learning. Doctoral research has vindicated the power of the modular system of education as a learning method, but it is the transformed learners themselves that give the system its credibility.

Watching the impact of Modules in action confirmed what I had long believed – if you give the locus of responsibility to learners and couple it with a framework for their progress, they will tend to amaze you. When years later I jotted down my kitchen-table epiphany of the HOT Plan for Pitsco, I wasn't consciously reflecting on what I had seen in observing the Modules system at work, but there is no doubt that it influenced me deeply.

Lessons in Church

Having a great culture in an organization is about providing a vision that people can make their own. But people can't take ownership of a vision if it is so big that they can't get their head around it. A few years ago I had cause to reflect on that fact while attending a meeting at my church.

People can't take ownership of a vision if it is too difficult to grasp.

Over time, many in the congregation had come to feel that our outreach program had begun to stagnate. The pastor had sent me a letter in January inviting me to participate in a discussion about potential outreach opportunities that the church might be missing. The letter had gone to 15 or so other people as well. On the night of the meeting, they arranged the tables for a big group powwow. We were divided into groups of six or seven. There was a good energy in the room. Everyone was ready to think big. But inside I felt a little trepidation, because I already knew what I was going to say and I knew the reaction it likely would get.

The minister was in charge. He passed out sheets of paper – two to each table. One of them had a list of the ministries in which the church was involved. I remember looking down at that list. There were probably 40 ministries written there. And the question he asked us was direct.

"What additional outreach ministries should we be doing?" the pastor asked. "We need original ideas – not bases we already have covered."

This was an enthusiastic crowd and pretty soon the people at my table were in a lively discussion. Ideas were flying about our table like popcorn kernels in a sizzling kettle. A young woman jotting speedily on a notepad was responsible for capturing all of these ideas and summarizing them to the larger group. But throughout the buzz, I didn't say a thing.

After a spell of this, the young woman looked up from her pad and said, "Harvey, you've been awfully quiet. What do you think?"

I paused a moment and then I said, "You don't want to know what I think."

"Yes we do! We want everyone's input," she protested.

"OK," I said, "but I'm going to be opposite to everyone. I'm not going to be popular."

The people sitting around the table gave me a quizzical look, but they wanted to know where I was coming from, so I explained myself.

"We've hatched a lot of ideas tonight – serious ideas, good ones. But my goodness, we already have 40 outreach programs," I said. "And we aren't doing so hot on some of those. We don't need any more. Instead of adding, we need to start drawing lines through ones we already have. We need to quit telling ourselves we are doing well at all of this when we really aren't."

After that they didn't ask me much.

When the table discussions wrapped up, the young woman stood up to deliver the results. She listed all the ideas the group came up with, several of which were clever and noble. "We think we ought to do this," she said, and "We think we ought to do that."

Then – she was a very nice young woman – she kind of smiled and said, "Except for Harvey. Harvey thinks we ought to get rid of about half of what we are doing and not add anything else."

At first there was a feeling of shock in the room. Then the pastor asked considerately which programs I thought we ought to get rid of. Honestly, I didn't really know. But I was sure of one thing.

"People don't own all of these," I said. "They can't. There are too many things to do and no system to manage getting them done. Until you have a system to get them done and a manageable number of ministries, we won't have people taking responsibility over the ventures we already have."

The pastor asked, "So how would you fix it?"

I teased around a little bit.

"I hate to say this," I said, "because it will mean work and I don't want a job."

He smiled at me and handed me the marker anyway. I walked up to the white board where the names of 40 current ministries were written.

"Here's what I think we have to do," I said. "Now, we all have to be in on it together, it won't be easy, and if you disagree with me I won't be offended. But what I think is that we need to develop a whole new plan."

First, I suggested that we pare the number of goals written on the white board down to a manageable number. It is easy to get starry-eyed and list 40 goals, but you have to pull back from this tendency. Instead of 40 goals, try 15, or even just eight. But not 40. People are finite creatures and they can only give themselves to so much at a time.

"Also, we need to divide into teams that are responsible for different ventures and create a system of targets that clearly spell out who is going to do what, by when, and what evidence there will be that it has been accomplished," I said. "Then we will know when these ministry goals have been met."

In addition, I explained, having a culture of accountability means that you discuss progress as a group, and too many commitments will dilute the focus – and the potency – of these discussions.

"Really," I said, "this amounts to transparency, because when things get too complex it muddies the water. You want a situation where everyone has a clear view of what everyone else is doing. That keeps work moving along more efficiently."

We talked awhile and I made my case. We set up another meeting and together came up with a shortened list of outreach opportunities, which we printed on forms. The next time the whole congregation was together, the forms were distributed and people were asked to consider which opportunities were for them. The program went on to find success and rejuvenated the spirit of our church's outreach campaign.

Throughout this process, the HOT Plan principles were at work. Limiting the number of ministries to those we could be effective with was our Must Win Challenge, the shortened list of outreach opportunities became the Key Initiatives, and the specific plans developed to carry out the ministries became the HOT Targets (HOTs). The process of distributing the forms to seek interest in and set up leadership for the fewer, more specific group of ministries moved the locus of responsibility from the pastor to those who must carry out the task, the people. In the context of churches and volunteer-based organizations, the HOT Plan is perhaps even more transformative than in the world of business. Because faith-based and volunteer organizations dedicate themselves to serving God and others, the HOT Plan, in this context, becomes a powerful facilitator of inspiration.

The Values of Success

You've come along with me as I have described my pursuit of an ideal company – one in which transferring the locus of responsibility is the key for success.

The stories in this chapter go beyond the world of business and show how the HOT Plan leads to superior results in various contexts. The principles at work in the HOT Plan are universal: the power of ownership and accountability, the importance of clarity and purpose, and loyalty to those you depend on and those who depend on you.

The HOT Plan empowers people to take ownership of success.

It bears repeating that everywhere a worthy vision exists, a HOT Plan can and will empower your people to take ownership of its success. This program is the best way I know to activate the collective power of personal responsibility in your organization and to focus it toward the accomplishment of your company's vision.

During the writing of this book, we celebrated our January HOT Check party for the 18th time. The HOT Check amount has grown from that first $92 to more than $1,800 per employee now. The annual HOT Check party has become a great day of celebration for our company. At this celebration we not only discover the amount of our bonus check but also see the big picture of our company's impact on education – our world – in the past year.

The HOT Plan respects the dignity of the people who work for you.

This year's big picture did not disappoint us. Even in a year of incredible transition for the company, more than three million students and teachers were served by Pitsco educational products, and more than 50 community organizations were helped through our giving and cultural HOTs. Our employees accomplished 91 percent of their HOTs – targets that included curriculum development for students, professional development for educators, and hands-on education for kids. We also developed 30 new products and published two inaugural catalogs, our first dedicated elementary catalog and the first *TETRIX Robotics* catalog. Our established departments continued their excellent work with publishing magazines, newsletters, videos, and social media interactions; manufacturing products with greater efficiency; expanding sales territories; and providing industry-leading customer service.

Without the HOT Plan, none of this would be possible.

The HOT Plan works. The HOT Plan works not because it is a slick new idea about how to get the most out of your employees, but because it respects the essential dignity and intelligence of the people who work for you.

I am convinced that there is a natural desire for significance in all people – a desire to do something extraordinary with their lives. The

HOT Plan taps into that deep desire for significance and paves the way for your employees to do extraordinary things together, united behind the vision of your company or organization. With a HOT Plan in place, the people of your organization have the confidence and tools necessary to visualize – and accomplish – the remarkable.

Appendices

I. Chapter Annotations

II. HOT Team Meeting Templates

III. Assigning HOT Points

IV. The Playbook

V. Recommended Resources

VI. Research Project: Culture Studies

Chapter Annotations

Chapter 1: Opportunity Knocks

[1] Brashears, L. (2012). "Culture Is a Business Issue." *Venture Capital Review*, 28, 55-60.

Chapter 2: Culture Happens

[2] Mosley, R. (2014). *Employer Brand Management: Practical Lessons from the World's Leading Employers* (1st ed.). Wiley: West Sussex, United Kingdom.

[3] Connors, R., & Smith, T. (2011). *Change the Culture, Change the Game: The Breakthrough Strategy for Energizing Your Organization and Creating Accountability for Results.* Portfolio Penguin: New York.

[4] Toossi, M. (2012). *Labor Force Projections to 2020: A More Slowly Growing Workforce.* Retrieved August 1, 2014.

[5] *PwC's NextGen: A Global Generational Study.* (2013). PricewaterhouseCoopers. University of Southern California and the London Business School.

[6] Gualtieri, W., & Seppanen, S. (2012). *The Millennial Generation Research Review.* US Chamber of Commerce Foundation.

[7] Pontefract, D. (2013). *Flat Army: Creating a Connected and Engaged Organization.* Jossey-Bass: San Francisco.

[8] *PwC's NextGen: A Global Generational Study.* (2013). PricewaterhouseCoopers. University of Southern California and the London Business School.

[9] *PwC's NextGen: A Global Generational Study.* (2013). PricewaterhouseCoopers. University of Southern California and the London Business School.

[10] Gualtieri, W., & Seppanen, S. (2012). *The Millennial Generation Research Review.* US Chamber of Commerce Foundation.

Chapter 3: Ownership Matters

[11] Kamen, D. (n.d.). Vision & Mission. Retrieved February 16, 2015, from http://www.usfirst.org/aboutus/vision.

[12] Pink, D. (2009). *Drive: The Surprising Truth About What Motivates Us.* Riverhead Books: New York.

[13] Stanhope, P. (2004). *Chesterfield's Letters to His Son*, PG Edition. [Project Gutenberg e-book]. Retrieved May 9, 2016, from http://www.gutenberg.org/files/3361/3361-h/3361-h.htm#link2H_4_0004. Produced by David Widger.

[14] *Online Etymology Dictionary.* (n.d.). Retrieved February 18, 2015, from http://www.etymonline.com/index.php?term=encourage.

Chapter 5: Success Shared

[15] *PwC's NextGen: A Global Generational Study.* (2013). PricewaterhouseCoopers. University of Southern California and the London Business School.

Chapter 6: HOT Evolution

[16] Keller, S., & Price, C. (2011). *Beyond Performance: How Great Organizations Build Ultimate Competitive Advantage.* Wiley: Hoboken, New Jersey.

[17] Lencioni, P. (2012). *The Advantage: Why Organizational Health Trumps Everything Else in Business*, 5. Jossey-Bass: San Francisco.

[18] Lencioni, P. (2012). *The Advantage: Why Organizational Health Trumps Everything Else in Business*, 193. Jossey-Bass: San Francisco.

Chapter 7: HOT Teams

[19] Katzenbach, J., & Smith, D. (1993). *The Wisdom of Teams: Creating the High-Performance Organization*, 45. Harvard Business School Press: Boston.

[20] Katzenbach, J., & Smith, D. (1993). *The Wisdom of Teams: Creating the High-Performance Organization*, 15. Harvard Business School Press: Boston.

[21] Towers Watson. (2012, July). *2012 Global Workforce Study: Engagement at Risk: Driving Strong Performance in a Volatile Global Environment* [Scholarly project].

[22] Parker, G., McAdams, J., & Zielinski, D. (2000). *Rewarding Teams: Lessons from the Trenches*. Jossey-Bass: San Francisco.

Chapter 8: HOT Targets

[23] *PwC's NextGen: A Global Generational Study.* (2013). PricewaterhouseCoopers. University of Southern California and the London Business School.

Chapter 9: HOT Accountability

[24] Connors, R., & Smith, T. (2004). *The Oz Principle: Getting Results Through Individual and Organizational Accountability* (Rev. and updated edition), 177. Portfolio: New York.

[25] National Association of Realtors® Research Division. (2012). *Social Benefits of Homeownership and Stable Housing*, 1-16. [White paper]. National Association of Realtors®.

[26] Crawford, M. (2009). *Shop Class as Soulcraft: An Inquiry into the Value of Work.* Penguin Press: New York.

[27] Crawford, M. (2009). *Shop Class as Soulcraft: An Inquiry into the Value of Work*, 60. Penguin Press: New York.

[28] Crawford, M. (2009). *Shop Class as Soulcraft: An Inquiry into the Value of Work*, 142. Penguin Press: New York.

Chapter 10: HOT Champion

[29] Champion, definition. (n.d.). Retrieved March 3, 2015, from http://dictionary.reference.com/browse/Champion?s=t.

Chapter 11: HOT Coaches

[30] Landry, T. (n.d.). "The secret to winning is constant, consistent management." Retrieved January 10, 2015, from http://www.azquotes.com/author/8459-Tom_Landry.

Chapter 13: HOT Data

[31] All About Watersheds. (n.d.). Retrieved May 29, 2015, from http://allaboutwatersheds.org.

[32] Structurational Theory: Social structures are the medium of human activities. (n.d.). Retrieved April 27, 2015, from https://www.utwente.nl/cw/theorieenoverzicht/Theory Clusters/Organizational Communication/Structurational_Theory

[33] Peterson, N. (Director) (2013 January 1). HOT Numbers. Annual HOT Check report. Lecture conducted from Pitsco, Inc., Pittsburg, KS.

[34] Sirisetti, S. (2012). "Employee Engagement Culture." *The Journal of Commerce*, 4(1), 72-74. Retrieved February 25, 2015.

[35] O.C. Tanner Company (2014). *The ROI of Effective Recognition.* [White paper]. Retrieved February 27, 2015.

[36] Sirisetti, S. (2012). "Employee Engagement Culture." *The Journal of Commerce*, 4(1), 72. Retrieved February 25, 2015.

[37] Peterson, N. (Director) (2016 January 1). HOT Numbers. Annual HOT Check report. Lecture conducted from Pitsco, Inc., Pittsburg, KS.

[38] Irwin, T. (2012 December 5). "Embedding Employee Engagement." *Mondaq Business Briefing*. Retrieved February 20, 2015.

[39] Kaufman, T., Chapman, T., & Allen, J. (2013). "The Effect of Performance Recognition on Employee Engagement," 1-17. [Working paper]. Cicero Group.

[40] Giddens, A. (1984). *The Constitution of Society: Outline of the Theory of Structuration*. Polity Press: Cambridge.

[41] Liston, C. (2015 April 29). "Organizational Structure and Organizational Culture: The Impact of the HOT Plan™ in Shaping a Highly Engaged Employee Culture at Pitsco, Inc." Pittsburg State University.

[42] Liston, C. (2015 May 7). "Organizational Structure and
    Organizational Culture: A Quantitative Measure of the Impact
    of the HOT Plan™ in Shaping a Highly Engaged Employee
    Culture at Pitsco, Inc." Pittsburg State University.

[43] Sirisetti, S. (2012). "Employee Engagement Culture." *The
    Journal of Commerce*, 4(1), 72-74. Retrieved February 25,
    2015.

[44] Irwin, T. (2012 December 5). "Embedding Employee
    Engagement." *Mondaq Business Briefing*. Retrieved February
    20, 2015.

Chapter 14: HOT Vision

[45] Hayes, K. (2008). *The Road to Monticello: The Life and Mind of
    Thomas Jefferson*, 91. Oxford University Press: Oxford.

[46] Owen, G. (2010). *The Rise and Fall of Great Companies:
    Courtaulds and the Reshaping of the Man-Made Fibres
    Industry*. Oxford University Press: Oxford.

Chapter 15: HOT Success

[47] US Department of Labor. "Entrepreneurship and the U.S.
    Economy." (n.d.). Retrieved March 3, 2015, from
    http://www.bls.gov/bdm/entrepreneurship/bdm_chart3.htm.

HOT Team Meeting Template

HOT Team Recorder: Responsibilities, Minutes Template, Guidelines

Each HOT Team must have a recorder, a critical role on the team. The recorder's minutes document the team's actions and decisions in every meeting. These minutes, in essence, become a living document that serves as a reference point on the progress toward completion of the HOT Targets. Minutes should be sent out within 48 hours of the meeting to all team members, to the executive team.

Here is a complete picture of the recorder's responsibilities:

Recorder Responsibilities
- Attend meetings
- Document actions and conclusions
- Collect fines
- Type up and distribute minutes using the standard meeting template

Standard Minutes Template
All minutes must follow the same format.
1) Team name
2) Meeting date
3) Team mission statement
4) Meeting #
5) Start time
6) End time
7) Members present

8) Members absent
9) Fines collected
10) YTD fines collected
11) Team leader welcome
12) Old business: Action items brought forward from previous meetings (Chart: List item, who is responsible, due date of project, and expected completion date for this item)
13) New business: Agenda items (Discussion notes, resolution or create a new action item)
14) New action items (Chart: List item, who is responsible, due date of project, and expected completion date for this item)
15) Next meeting information – day, date, time, and location for next meeting
16) Prepared and submitted by: (name of recorder)

Notes
- Any action items should be listed in red with a date to be completed. Dates are very important.
- At the end of the minutes, all action items should be stated again with responsibilities and due dates.
- Keep minutes to two pages or less per hour of meeting if possible.
- Minutes should be sent out within 48 hours of the meeting to all team members and copied to the executive team.
- Collected fines should be given to a designated person.
- Consider creating a shared online folder for team documents. Provide a link to the folder instead of attaching multiple files to the outgoing email.

Insert company logo here.

Team Name_____
Meeting Date_____

Put the team mission statement here.

	Members:					
Mtg #						
Start Time						
End Time						
Meeting Fines						
YTD Fines						

X=present; E=excused; blank=absent

Welcome

The team captain welcomed the team and updated them on…

Old Business

Action Items from previous meeting

Action Items	Responsible	Due Date	Expected Completion

New Business

Agenda Item 1
- Discussion
- Resolution (or Action Item)

Agenda Item 2
- Discussion
- Resolution (or Action Item)

Agenda Item 3 [Continue agenda items as needed]
- Discussion
- Resolution (or Action Item)

Action Items

Action Items	Responsible	Due Date	Expected Completion

Minutes prepared by [YOUR NAME]. The next meeting will be held on [DAY], [DATE] at [TIME, A.M./P.M.] in the [LOCATION].

Assigning HOT Points

As mentioned in Chapter 8, the following chart is used to determine HOT Points. This chart is available on our company intranet so that any employee, team, or department can access this information and use it for planning at any time.

A word of encouragement is in order here; posting this chart (and other similar resources) in a shared space in your office where your employees can easily see it, or on an employee intranet site, provides a great boost for your workplace culture! Transparency builds trust and also motivates teams to plan well. Every time you make your processes more accessible and transparent to your employees, you increase trust throughout your organization.

HOT Points:

Time to Complete	Points
8 hours or less	2
9-16 hours	3
17-40 hours	4
41-80 hours	5
81-120 hours	6
121-160 hours	8
1-3 months	10
3-6 months	12
All year	15

The Playbook

Creating greater efficiency with the HOT Plan management is a process of continuous improvement. The HOT Plan is flexible enough to allow for updates to record-keeping processes that make it easier to keep the HOT Plan on target each year. Pitsco's executive leadership team has made several updates over the years.

One of our recent updates has been the creation of an annual, one-page playbook for the leadership team, Tribal Council. The playbook is a handy tool that can be used over the next 12 months as a guide for day-to-day decision making. The playbook increases clarity by answering six essential questions that can guide decisions through reviewing company priorities.

At the first of each year, the playbook is printed, laminated, and sized to fit inside the front cover of a standard-size journal. A laminated copy of the playbook is kept inside the front or back cover of all Tribal Council members' journal/calendars so they can refer to it easily.

Below is a copy of a Pitsco playbook.

Pitsco Education Playbook 2015

1. **Why do we exist?** To make a difference in the lives of learners around the world.
2. **How do we behave?** Dedicated, loyal, customer-centric
3. **What do we do?** We develop, manufacture, and market hands-on educational products, curriculum, and services for learners.
4. **How will we succeed? (Must Win Challenges)**
   - Increased financial performance (revenue by x%, profitability by x%)

- Provide relevant, effective products and standards-based curriculum
- Hire and develop employees who embrace Pitsco values

5. What is most important, right now?

Thematic Goal – Expand STEM presence

Defining Objectives

- Develop and actualize STEM sales and marketing plan
- Grow and strengthen relationships with STEM partners
- Identify champion to create STEM curriculum analytics plan
- Analyze and update STEM portfolio
  - o 3-D Printing
  - o Robotics
  - o Professional Development
  - o Elementary

Standard Operating Objectives (MWCs)

- Increase revenue and profitability
- Develop products that meet academic standards
- Target new customers with coordinated sales and marketing plans
- Seek and strengthen partnerships
- Acquire and implement business analytics

6. Who must do what?

Name	Title	General Responsibilities
Lisa	President	Lead the development, management, and implementation of strategic initiatives, coordination of resources, and internal communication.
Robin	Vice President	Lead revenue generation through the development, management, and implementation of sales efforts.
Matt	Vice President	Lead the Customer Experience Team from presale Program Design through post-sale Professional Services.
Nancy	Director of Educator Insights	Lead the delivery of insights for data-driven decision making.
Dave	Director of Curriculum Development	Develop and lead an organization that will design, create, and improve our curriculum in an efficient and effective manner, blending on-site employees, contractors, and partners together smoothly.
Kyle	Director of Manufacturing	Lead, develop, and manage the strategic initiatives of Manufacturing and fulfillment of proprietary products.
Scott	Director of Operations	Lead, direct, and implement the supply chain through partnerships, strategic initiatives, and established KPIs.

Recommended Resources

Books

The Advantage: Why Organizational Health Trumps Everything Else in Business, by Patrick Lencioni. Jossey-Bass: San Francisco, 2012.

The Alliance: Managing Talent in the Networked Age, by Reid Hoffman, with Ben Casnocha and Chris Yeh. Harvard Business Review Press: New York, 2014.

Blue Ocean Strategy: How to Create Uncontested Market Space and Make the Competition Irrelevant, by W. Chan Kim and Renée Mauborgne. Harvard Business School Publishing Corporation: Boston, 2015.

The Carrot Principle: How the Best Managers Use Recognition to Engage Their People, Retain Talent, and Accelerate Performance, second edition, by Adrian Gostick and Chester Elton. Free Press: New York, 2009.

Flat Army: Creating a Connected and Engaged Organization, by Dan Pontefract. Jossey-Bass: San Francisco, 2013.

Good to Great, by Jim Collins. HarperCollins Publishers: New York, 2001.

Great by Choice: Uncertainty, Chaos, and Luck – Why Some Thrive Despite Them All, by Jim Collins and Morton T. Hansen. HarperCollins Publishers: New York, 2011.

HBR's 10 Must Reads: The Essentials (Organizational Development). *Harvard Business Review*, Peter F. Drucker, Clayton M. Christensen, Michael E. Porter, Daniel Goleman. Harvard Business Review Press: Boston, November 2008.

Helping People Win at Work: A Business Philosophy Called "Don't Mark My Paper, Help Me Get an A," by Ken Blanchard and Garry Ridge. Pearson Education: Upper Saddle River, New Jersey, 2009.

The Monster Under the Bed: How Business Is Mastering the Opportunity of Knowledge for Profit, by Stan Davis and Jim Botkin. Touchstone: New York, 1994.

Multipliers: How the Best Leaders Make Everyone Smarter, by Liz Wiseman with Greg McKeown. HarperCollins Publishers: New York, 2010.

Organizational Culture and Leadership, by Edgar Schein. Sage Publications: Thousand Oaks, California, 2004.

The Power of Mentoring: Shaping People Who Will Shape the World, by Martin Sanders, with foreword by Leighton Ford. WingSpread Publishers: Camp Hill, Pennsylvania, 2009.

The Wisdom of Teams: Creating the High-Performance Organization, by Jon R. Katzenbach and Douglas K. Smith. McKinsey & Company: New York, 1993.

Software

HOTware™ is the HOT Plan tracking software developed by Pitsco, Inc. This target-tracking software automates point tracking for the HOT Plan in your business and maintains transparency with employees by posting a running total of targets and point totals on the company intranet or employee website pages. It is soon to be available for purchase from Pitsco, Inc.

Additional Studies and Articles

Aisha, A., Hardjomidjojo, P., & Yassierli (2013). "Effects of Working Ability, Working Condition, Motivation and Incentive on Employees Multi-Dimensional Performance." *International Journal of Innovation, Management and Technology*, 4(6), 605.

Brown, D.I. (1995). "Team-Based Reward Plans." *Team Performance Management*, 1(1), 23-31.

Brashears, L. (2012). "Culture Is a Business Issue." *Venture Capital Review*, 28, 55-60.

Curşeu, P., Janssen, S., & Meeus, M. (2014). "Shining Lights and Bad Apples: The Effect of Goal-Setting on Group Performance." *Management Learning*, 45(3), 332-348.

Devlin, B. (2012). "Collaborative Business Intelligence: Socializing Team-Based Decision Making." *Business Intelligence Journal*, 17(3), 9-17.

Dow, G.K. (1998). "Configurational and Coactivational Views of Organizational Structure." *Academy of Management Review*, 13(1), 53-64.

Irwin, T. (2012). "Embedding Employee Engagement." *Mondaq Business Briefing*.

Janićijević, N. (2011). "Methodological Approaches in the Research of Organizational Culture." *Economic Annals*, LVI (189), 69-100.

Janićijević, N. (2013). "The Mutual Impact of Organizational Culture and Structure." *Economic Annals*, LVIII (198), 35-60.

Kaufman, T. & Chapman, T. Cicero Group. (2012). "The Effect of Years of Service Awards Programs." [White paper].

Kaufman, T., & Chapman, T. Cicero Group. (2012). "Optimizing Employee Recognition Programs." [White paper].

Kaufman, T., Chapman, T., & Allen, J. Cicero Group. (2013). "The Effect of Performance Recognition on Employee Engagement." [White paper].

Kolk, A., & Perego, P. (2014). "Sustainable Bonuses: Sign of Corporate Responsibility or Window Dressing?" *Journal of Business Ethics*, 119(1), 1-15.

Nawab, S., Bhatti, K., & Shafi, K. (2011). "Effect of Motivation on Employees Performance." *Interdisciplinary Journal of Contemporary Research in Business*, 3(3), 1209-1216.

Nolan, S. (2011). "Employee Engagement." *Strategic HR Review*, 10(3), 3-4.

O.C. Tanner Company. (2014). *The ROI of Effective Recognition.* [White paper].

Park, R. & Kruse, D. (2014). "Group Incentives and Financial Performance: The Moderating Role of Innovation." *Human Resource Management Journal*, 24(1), 77-94.

PwC's NextGen: A Global Generational Study: Evolving Talent Strategy to Match the New Workforce Reality. (2013). PricewaterhouseCoopers. University of Southern California and the London Business School.

Sirisetti, S. (2012). "Employee Engagement Culture." *The Journal of Commerce*, 4(1), 72-74.

Trahant, B. (2009). "Driving Better Performance Through Continuous Employee Engagement." *Public Manager*, 38(1), 54-58.

Towers Watson. (2012). *2012 Global Workforce Study: Engagement at Risk: Driving Strong Performance in a Volatile Global Environment.*

From the Original Research Project I – Qualitative Culture Study

Organizational Structure and Organizational Culture: The impact of the HOT Plan™ *in shaping a highly engaged employee culture at Pitsco, Inc.*

- A qualitative study conducted by Carole K. Liston, a graduate student at Pittsburg State University, Pittsburg, Kansas, April 29, 2015

Overview

In 1997, Pittsburg, Kansas-based Pitsco, Inc., an innovative STEM education company and creator of education products and curriculum, hit a slump in its company culture that stymied its success and threatened to close its doors, according to Pitsco founder and CEO Harvey Dean.

Instead, the structure of the company was radically redesigned by Dean through a system he calls the HOT Plan™, and his company did an about-face. Over the next 17 years – from 1997 to 2014 – the numbers of educators and students served by Pitsco dramatically increased; in fact, by 2013 the number of students and teachers served had increased by over 230 percent, reaching over 9.3 million that year.[48] Dean believes the key to the successful turnaround was in changing the company's culture and that the HOT Plan accomplished this by first changing the organizational structure. Indeed, the HOT Plan changed Pitsco's structure from a hierarchal top-down model – in which all decisions and assignments originate from the top of the corporate hierarchy – to a more flat, adaptive business model guided by an executive leadership team and carried out by interdepartmental and departmental teams. The HOT Plan also creates opportunity for employee input from all levels and grants employees the locus of responsibility for completing their work.

Put simply, the HOT Plan worked. Since 1996-97, the culture has transformed from a negative, fragmented workplace in danger of losing key leadership to a highly engaged, unified employee culture that is laser focused on the company's strategic priorities, according to Dean. Dean offers *The HOT Plan*, with step-by-step instructions, in hopes that other companies will experience success with this plan as well.

But is this realistic? Change is a complex process that depends on many factors. Is the success of the HOT Plan unique to Pitsco's particular blend of leadership personality and small-business, Midwestern values, or can a HOT Plan change in how things are done (structure) actually transform any company's or organization's culture?

The Structuration Theory of Organizational Communication

According to the Structuration Theory of Organizational Communication, developed by British sociologist Anthony Giddens, the idea that culture and structure interact and change each other has sound basis in the nature of human beings and how they interact with the world around them. Giddens theorizes, in fact, that organizational structure and organizational culture never exist separately from each other. Instead, the two share a duality of structure.[49] In other words, like Dean believes, Giddens says that the two are intertwined; they influence each other; they are dynamic cocreators.

Dean's idea that the HOT Plan has not only reshaped Pitsco's culture but can also create unified, high-engagement cultures in other businesses and organizations finds a strong foundation in Giddens' Structuration Theory. Dean developed a hypothesis that the change in organizational structure by the HOT Plan has produced the highly engaged employee culture of Pitsco.

A Qualitative Study

To test Dean's hypothesis, we first looked to other literature on employee engagement and reviewed 32 sources, including one study that reviewed 146 cases to examine the impact of financial incentives on work performance.[50] We then conducted qualitative research through interviews with 10 Pitsco employees, who ranged in age from 30 to 61 years and ranged in tenure with the company from 18 months to 24 years.

A Sampling of Interview Findings: Employee Engagement

When asked to define a highly engaged employee, over half the participants said that the definition must include the idea that the employee puts the good of the company ahead of his or her personal career goals. JH, a 30-year-old male with over 10 years of tenure at Pitsco, believed this attitude is best indicated by actions, by someone who goes the second mile for the good of the company.

"A highly engaged and fully participating employee is one who gives himself to the company," JH says. "They just don't look at the company as they walk in and start the morning by punching their timecard, do their time, and punch their timecard on the way out at five o'clock. They are someone who is willing to take the extra steps, you know, stay a little later if necessary."

A strong work ethic and the ability to see the company's vision, or the big picture, were also named by most participants as defining elements of high employee engagement. JD, a 36-year-old female with over 10 years of tenure at the company, said simply that a highly engaged employee is one "who really cares." MO, an employee with more than two decades experience at Pitsco, pointed out that "acting like an owner" is essential to employee engagement.

DR, a 37-year-old male with over 10 years of tenure, believed instead that the organizational structure of the company was paramount to engagement.

"[Engagement is created by] the company investing and caring and showing the employee that that they do care about them, either by incentives or things like quality insurance and quality culture around them," DR said.

Employee Engagement at Pitsco

In relationship to Pitsco specifically, participants were asked a similar question: "On a scale of one to seven with seven being the highest, how would you rank employee engagement at Pitsco?"

Half the group – a group composed of both sexes, millennials and non-millennials – rated Pitsco's employee engagement at a six. Of the rest, two ranked Pitsco employee engagement at a seven, two ranked it at a five, and one gave Pitsco's employee engagement the low ranking of four.

The HOT Plan and Employee Engagement

Ten out of 10 participants said the HOT Plan positively affects employee engagement at Pitsco. Although one saw the HOT goals (Targets) as "over and above" the regular workload and therefore somewhat onerous, seven out of 10 believed the HOT Plan structure increases employee engagement.

"I can tell you from experience that the HOT Plan is one of the keys (to employee engagement at Pitsco)," said RB, a 61-year-old male, an employee at Pitsco for over 10 years. "Everybody goes with the HOT Plan kicking and screaming every step of the way; we're all busy, and then here comes HOT goals. But somehow, some way they help us see the big picture. I think that's the key; you are forced to stop and think about the entirety of what you are doing."

The HOT Check also had support from 100 percent of those interviewed. Ten out of 10 participants stated that they believed the financial bonus was either essential or very important to make the HOT Plan realistic and effective to employees. Additionally, eight participants said the HOT Check is a motivational tool that keeps their HOT Targets (goals) on the radar throughout the year and helps them prioritize their work.

Support for the Hypothesis

Dean's hypothesis that the HOT Plan has shaped Pitsco's culture into a positive, highly engaged workplace was ultimately supported by the qualitative study of Pitsco's culture.

Enthusiasm, loyalty, job satisfaction, longevity of job tenure, and a willingness to go above-and-beyond what is required – all characteristics of highly engaged employees – were present in 100 percent of the respondents to the qualitative study. In addition, the steadily increasing number of students and teachers served since the HOT Plan was begun at Pitsco indicates increased profitability for the company as well.[51]

For additional insights, sources, and literature review analysis of the 2015 qualitative study, the original survey is available for purchase from Pitsco, Inc.

From the Original Research Project II – Quantitative Culture Study

Organizational Structure and Organizational Culture: A quantitative measure of the impact of the HOT Plan™ in shaping a highly engaged employee culture at Pitsco, Inc.

– A quantitative study conducted by Carole K. Liston, a graduate student at Pittsburg State University, Pittsburg, Kansas, May 7, 2015

An Overview of Quantitative Testing of the Pitsco Culture

Following the qualitative, interview-based study, we felt that Dean's hypothesis (the change in organizational structure by the HOT Plan has produced the highly engaged employee culture of Pitsco) needed a quantifiable, broader-based test. The next month after completing the qualitative research report in April 2015, we followed it with a broader spectrum quantitative study on the company culture using the instrument of an online survey.

To measure and quantify a broader spectrum of the culture of Pitsco, we turned to a standardized measure of organizational culture known as the Organizational Culture Survey (OCS) first published in 1987 by Glaser, Zamanou, and Hacker.[52] The OCS is composed of 36 statements in six subsets, and participants choose from answers that range from "Strongly Agree" to "Strongly Disagree" on a five-part Likert-type scale. Since OCS culture statements are worded positively, to select "Agree" or "Strongly Agree" as answers indicates employee satisfaction with the company culture.

Methodology for the Quantitative Study

Research Site

Research was conducted on the main campus of Pitsco, Inc. in Pittsburg, Kansas. Pitsco, Inc. was founded in Pittsburg, Kansas, in 1971 and moved to its current home at 915 E Jefferson Street in Pittsburg in 1977. The Jefferson Street campus houses the corporate offices of Pitsco, including the executive leadership team; Accounting; Human Resources; Communications (publications, news releases, editing); research; IT; new media and Marketing; Curriculum and Product Development; the Call Center; and Shipping and Receiving.

The main campus is home base for 152 of Pitsco's 190 employees. Pitsco's remaining employees work offsite, either at the Pittsburg-based manufacturing facility at 106 W 4th Street or as regional employees of various types around the country. Because the survey was testing the cultural impact of the HOT Plan's organizational structure, only employees on the main campus – who have relatively the same exposure to the HOT Plan and its supporting mechanisms – were surveyed.

Participants and Procedures

The survey was conducted under the guidance of Pitsco employees Nancy Peterson, director of educator insights, and Stephanie Manes, research coordinator. Surveys were emailed to all employees on-campus at Jefferson Street.

The survey was sent out from the researcher instead of the Pitsco survey department to reinforce anonymity. Over the three-day period, the survey was emailed to all employees on the main campus 4 times. There were 87 opt-in responses and 82 surveys completed. Of the 82 participants who completed valid surveys, 33 identified as male and 49 identified as female.

How the Survey Was Administered at Pitsco

The survey was administered through the company email via Survey Monkey. It was distributed via a link sent out with an email inviting participation. Completed survey responses were exported from Survey Monkey into a format compatible with SPSS (.sav files). Exported files were uploaded into SPSS at Pittsburg State University, where they were analyzed under distribution frequencies, in a sex-based T-test and a tenure-based Anova test.

Findings

Frequencies
Statistics (Number of Respondents, Overall Participation)

Statistical analysis of the survey in frequency distribution reveals that 87 employees responded to the opt-out question, with 83 "yes" answers and four "no" answers, a 95.4 percent positive response rate for participation. Of these 83 responses, 82 respondents completed the survey, with 33 respondents identifying themselves as male and 49 respondents identifying themselves as female. This same group number remained active for the tenure questions. In answer to the question "How long have you worked at Pitsco?," the group broke down as follows:

- 5 years or less – 39
- 6-10 years – 19
- 11-15 years – 6
- 16-20 years – 4
- 21+ years – 14

Statistical Significance/Standard Deviation

Results from the male/female-based T-test reveal only one answer of statistical significance. The statement "My supervisor takes criticism well" reported with a two-tailed significance of <.05 percent. This statistic is accentuated when compared to the differing male/female mean on the same question, with a mean for males at 4.28 and a mean for females of 3.98. This statistical difference indicates that the males and females taking this test experience confrontation with their supervisor differently when reflecting criticism *from the employee to the supervisor*.

Results from the one-way Anova test, based on employee tenure in five categories also revealed no significant statistical difference between tenure groups in the reflection of the organizational culture at Pitsco.

The Significance of Sameness:

Combining Percentage of "Agree" and "Strongly Agree" Answers

Since the Pitsco survey seeks to discover if high employee engagement is *embedded* in the culture, the researcher was looking for a consistency of experience: the significance of sameness. To judge this, we took note of the combined percentage of workers marking "Agree" and "Strongly Agree" on the survey.

This finding proved to be a significant way to view the data of the Pitsco survey. In each of the subsets, the number of employees and the percentage of respondents who filled out "Agree" and "Strongly Agree" were summed and charted. All 36 questions ranked at the 50th percentile and above when "Agree" and "Strongly Agree" answers were combined. The lowest "Agree" and "Strongly Agree" score given was 52% in the area of "Know what's happening in other work areas," and the highest score given was unanimous: 100 percent agreement with the statement "Supervisor gives criticism in positive manner."

Discussion

Dean's hypothesis that the HOT Plan's organizational structure has shaped Pitsco's culture appears to be supported by the quantitative survey in two ways. First, the virtual lack of statistical significance in the employee population who participated in the survey indicates a consistent cultural experience across the board. With the exception of the way that male and female respondents experience their supervisors in circumstances of employee-to-supervisor criticism, the culture is homogenous.

Second, out of the 36 statements rated, *only nine statements fell below the 80 percent line when categories "Agree" and "Strongly Agree" were combined*. Five of those nine statements occurred in the final subscale of the test (on Meetings), and though significant, factors of test fatigue must be considered in the final section of any long survey.

It should also be noted that the week prior to this survey being sent out, LEGO® Education, a contract partner of Pitsco that employs a significant number of Pitsco employees at the Jefferson Street campus, announced an unanticipated move of operations to Boston, Massachusetts. This means that the LEGO account jobs in Pittsburg, Kansas, will likely be lost. This was a blow to many local employees and no doubt influenced some of the lower scores given, including for "Understand reasons changes are made" and "Know what's happening in other work areas."

The company was ranked especially high by employees in areas of teamwork, high involvement, a sense of employee empowerment, job motivation, organizational commitment, and trust. These are all areas that indicate high employee engagement, according to Sirisetti.[53]

Conclusions

Support for the Hypothesis

As in the qualitative report, Giddens' Structuration Theory was again found to be a sound theoretical basis for Dean's hypothesis. The culture of Pitsco is marked by a sense of deep, caring commitment and collegiality among employees. This culture was resoundingly affirmed by employees at all levels of the organization in both the qualitative and quantitative studies of the company. It seems obvious that the trust and caring exhibited among employees is deeply embedded in the culture of Pitsco – a rich fruit of the company's core values, which are facilitated by the HOT Plan.

A Partial Listing of Sources for the 2015 Pitsco Culture Audit Research Project

[48] Peterson, N. (Director) (2013 January 1). HOT Numbers. Annual HOT Check report. Lecture conducted from Pitsco, Inc., Pittsburg, KS.

[49] Structurational Theory: Social structures are the medium of human activities. (n.d.). Retrieved April 27, 2015, from https://www.utwente.nl/cw/theorieenoverzicht/Theory Clusters/Organizational Communication/Structurational_Theory

[50] Garbers, Y., & Konradt, U. (2014). "The Effect of Financial Incentives on Performance: A Quantitative Review of Individual and Team-Based Financial Incentives." *Journal of Occupational and Organizational Psychology*, 87, 102-137.

[51] Peterson, N. (Director) (2013 January 1). HOT Numbers. Annual HOT Check report. Lecture conducted from Pitsco, Inc., Pittsburg, KS.

[52] Glaser, S.R., Zamanou, S., & Hacker, K. "Measuring and Interpreting Organizational Culture." *Management Communication Quarterly*, 1, 173-198.

[53] Sirisetti, S. (2012). "Employee Engagement Culture." *The Journal of Commerce*, 4(1), 72-74. Retrieved February 25, 2015.

ACKNOWLEDGMENTS

As one traverses through life, the influencers, examples, provokers of ideas, close friends, casual acquaintances, the unexpected overheard comments become a part of what makes up a life.

Many of these influences simmer in the soul; they incubate the "What ifs?" and the "Why nots?"; they encourage the wonderings of "Could it work?" All of Life's voices direct – and sometimes redirect – who one is, and who one become.

So when it came time to acknowledge those who have contributed to the formation of this book, *The HOT Plan*™, there is no small group to thank. Rather, the voices to whom I am indebted number in the thousands.

However, the kudos for the deep and guiding light of my life, and the ideals upon which this book is founded, go to my parents. Kudos go to Dad with his eighth-grade education, devout faith in God, and steady role in my sometimes erratic life. Kudos to Mom, a gentle soul devout in her love, who was crippled at 12 years of age but became a high school graduate along with only three others. She was a businesswoman, a provider of Avon products to the community for 25 years. Life as a son with this foundation of love, God, and practical day-to-day living has served me well. I am thankful.

ABOUT THE AUTHOR

Dr. Harvey Dean is recognized as an entrepreneur, educator, thought leader, and businessman.

As founder and CEO of Pitsco, Dean oversees Pitsco's operations as well as all Pitsco publications and catalogs. Pitsco is the leader in STEM education in the United States and the creator and distributor of TETRIX® Robotics Building Systems and manufactures over 500 hands-on education products. Pitsco's curriculum and training affect teachers and students in all 50 United States and in 53 countries around the world. More than 200 million students worldwide have used the innovative curriculum and products of Pitsco.

In 1993, Dean was chosen as a regional Entrepreneur of the Year by *Inc.* magazine. In 1997, he received a prestigious Small Press/IPPY book award for his book, *Changing Education*. He has received numerous other awards and is a sought-after speaker at education conferences and seminars.

He and his wife, Sharon, have three adult children and 11 grandchildren.

ADDITIONAL CONTRIBUTORS TO
THE HOT PLAN™

C.L. King: Cowriter, Researcher, Developmental Editor, Project Manager

Carole Lynn (C.L.) King is an award-winning professional writer, developmental editor, and media specialist who assisted the HOT Plan project in research, conceptual/developmental editing, writing, and project management. Her work on *The HOT Plan*™ received honors from Pittsburg State University (Pittsburg, Kansas) and the Communication Department as a thesis project for her MA in Communication. Carole is a seasoned professional writer and editor whose background includes business journalism, human interest stories and personality profiles, magazine features, marketing communications, and public relations. Carole lives with her family in Southwest Missouri.

Cody White: Cowriter, Developmental Editor

Cody White was instrumental in getting the HOT Plan project off the ground. Long before he ever dreamed of being involved in telling the HOT Plan's story, Cody experienced the HOT Plan as an employee of Pitsco, Inc. He later assisted with the initial research and writing for *The HOT Plan*. Cody continues his work as an editor, writer, and photographer for Pitsco, overseeing the company's internal newsletter and contributing to Pitsco's external publications and various other communication projects. Cody lives in Southwest Missouri.

Timothy Holden: Technical Editor

Timothy Holden is a student at Pittsburg State University, double majoring in Accounting and Music. As technical editor for *The HOT Plan*, Timothy formatted the manuscript for e-book and print publication, including all text, illustrations, and e-book links. Timothy graduates from PSU in December 2016.

Rodney Dutton: Illustrator, Cover Art

Rodney Dutton illustrated *The HOT Plan* and also produced the cover art and the concept design for the HOT Architecture chart in Chapter 6. Rodney is an award-winning illustrator known for his unique pencil sketch style in concept art. A businessman, artist, and educator, Rodney lives in Southeast Kansas and currently serves special needs students as an art instructor and therapist.

Andra Bryan Stefanoni: Literary Editor

Andra Bryan Stefanoni served as literary editor for *The HOT Plan*. Andra is an award-winning journalist whose work has ranged from compelling human interest stories to extensive coverage of the 2011 Joplin tornado. A lifelong resident of Southeast Kansas who comes from a family of educators, she is now a freelance writer and media communications specialist.

Todd McGeorge: Graphic Design

Todd McGeorge served as graphic designer for *The HOT Plan*'s cover and HOT Architecture chart. Todd has been a graphic designer on Pitsco's Marketing Team for over 20 years and has worked closely on the successful development and marketing of thousands of Pitsco products during that time.

Pitsco Editing Department

Pitsco's Editing Department provided editorial review and copyediting for *The HOT Plan* throughout the development of the book. Special thanks to Communications Manager Tom Farmer, Editing Coordinator Angie Henderson, and Technical Editor Matt Sluder for their helpful review of *The HOT Plan*.

www.ingramcontent.com/pod-product-compliance
Lightning Source LLC
Chambersburg PA
CBHW072117270326
41931CB00010B/1588